Radical Companies

WITHOUT BOSSES AND EMPLOYEES

Matt **PEREZ** | Adrian **PEREZ** | Jose **LEAL**

Businesses Are Broken and They Break People

This book is about what we call Radical Companies, owned and managed by the people who embody them and give them life. It is for people who want to make an impact on the world, not just to make money.

What has evolved into today's economy has worked relatively well for many of us, but has worked best for the powerful few. Without question, things have gotten better since the eighteenth century, but the playing field still tilts to the powerful and deep disparities continue today. By far, the biggest issue is not the wealth gap, but the fact that we accept it as inevitable. It's going to be difficult to do, but we have to shake off those habits that lead us to be so compliant with the way things are.

Today businesses are grounded on imposed hierarchy, fear, and separation. The American and French Revolutions eliminated the royalty as royalty, but left the landlords in charge of humanity's land. And that's where we've been stuck for a few hundred years. What we have to realize is that ownership by the few is not sacred, just like slavery is not sacred regardless of the Christian Bible.

We need to move on or we are going to slide deeper into a dystopian nightmare as fewer and fewer people wade in abundance while the rest drown in scarcity and fight for survival. We are living better off today. In fact, most people alive today live in financial splendor compared with the royalty of previous centuries. But that's only along the financial dimension.

On the other hand, we are definitely drowning in scarcity of time and choices. We are definitely stunted in our ability to live a full life. Most of the wealth is controlled by a handful of people.

This book is *not* about convincing you that there is a problem. If you are happy and satisfied with things as they are, you might want to skip reading the rest of this book and avoid being uncomfortable. We wrote this book for people who want to live in a more just world than the one we live in today. We wrote it for people who sense that things could be better for everybody. We wrote it for those who might have started but are now looking for what's next.

The change is in your hands. No complaining about it, or agitating for revolution, or hoping that a benevolent government will rescue us. We can help bring about a new paradigm of wealth and wellbeing. We have to focus to generate the impact that we want to see in the world.

This book is about making a more desirable future happen sooner rather than later.

A Healthy Society

We see companies as places where lots of exploration and experiments will take place. Companies are where people spend most of their waking hours and where they experience what *normal* is. As new habits and new ways of living not driven by fear take root in these companies, they will spread to our families, our schools, our societies, and beyond.

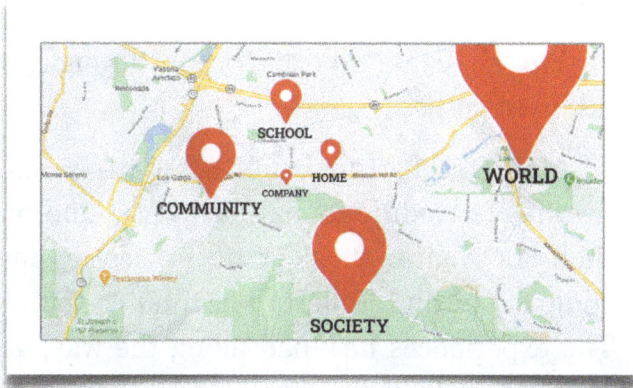

Organization

This book is organized in three parts, starting with Part One the story of a self-managed company, Nearsoft, and how it came about.

Part Two lays out the fundamental components of the Radical paradigm that will help us move away from the dead end that we are headed towards now.

Part Three lists out a bunch of use cases and examples of what we would do to create a company with decentralized ownership and collaborative management.

Speaking of Authors...

We all came to this point through very different paths.

Matt got to this point after 40 years of working in traditional fiat businesses and more than 14 years at Nearsoft, a co-managed company he and Roberto Martinez co-founded. The experiences he's had along the way, good and bad, underpin this book.

Adrian, like many of his generation, has always been uncomfortable with the because-I-say-so business world. He watched up close how an exciting start up collapsed after the bosses in charge led it down a dead end. In his own startups, he has experienced how difficult it is to make decisions without an explicit alignment mechanism.

Jose started several businesses while in his late teens, rode the Internet wave, and felt the bite of the very same grinder he had helped create. He got off that path and spent several years researching and studying what makes us humans and what prompts us to certain actions and choices. Much of that experience has shaped the work that has gone into this book.

Terminology

Fiat	Throughout the book we use the term Fiat, the power to give arbitrary orders.
Co-management, Co-Ownership	We put our own spin on co-management and co-ownership.
Bosses	We avoid confusing misnomers like CEO, executives, and managers, and euphemisms like leaders: we call them all bosses instead.
Business vs Companies	We differentiate company from business, corporation, cooperative, collaborative, etc. The latter all have to do with making capital. Company comes from the Latin *co-* (together) and *panis* (bread): a group of people who break bread together.

Part I
Our Fiat World

Once Upon a Time

As Gallup, ADP, and others have reported, disengagement is extremely high and a good chunk of people's lives is wasted *"at work."* Businesses know this, but they accept the bare minimum results in exchange for an illusion of control.

On the other hand, operating without bosses, or titles, or a ranked hierarchy sounds impossible. But it works. I've experienced it at Nearsoft, a self-managed company that Roberto Martinez and I founded in 2007.

But self-management is not enough.

For a sustainable solution, we need to address the issue of ownership. The oligarchic ownership of the past does not work for most of us anymore, we need a new model.

Companies

Companies are our economic engines. It's easy to understand the frustration that leads to the "*screw the corporation*" sentiment, but we wouldn't know what to replace them with. The communist regimes have tried to turn private businesses into public ones and have the government own them all. A centralized system that always end up as dictatorships.

Decentralized ownership is central to liberty, I know this from my own experience with the (Cuban) regime.

Appealing to "*the new man*" or our angelical side is not enough, probably because we don't have an angelical side. Or an evil side. Or any sides, we are just people.

Instead, we reimagined companies as places where people learn to manage their work collaboratively, without bosses, instead of today's "*because I say so (or else).*" Places where people can experience co-ownership (*i.e.*, decentralized ownership) instead of the Fiat ownership we've inherited. These we call these places Radical Companies.

For the Radical paradigm presented below we've tried to keep the things that make modern companies effective at bringing people together and at generating wealth. We've also removed the pieces that are obviously broken and make us miserable and instead point to ways to unlock our voices and spread that wealth according to contributors.

The Itch

In mid 2005, I started Nearsoft,[1] a business to help software product businesses grow their software development teams. By then, I had been involved with six hardware and software startups and I knew that growing an engineering team was getting harder. And it wasn't just me: many of my peers dealt with the same challenge.

I was already in my early 50s, so the prospect of looking for *a job* was not very appealing. Lucky me, I knew enough people in the business and could have eventually found a well-paying job with a grand-sounding title but it would be more of the same. I could not get excited about that prospect, so I kept trying to figure out other options.

I was having lunch with a buddy and we commiserated about working with body shops overseas, half a world away. In passing, I said something like, *"Doing this stuff on the other side of the world doesn't make sense—but if we could do this in Mexico, that would work great."*

Brain Worm

As I drove away, the idea of having a team in Mexico kept bouncing around in my head.

I had been outsourcing pieces of software product development to faraway places like India and Eastern Europe because everybody *knew* that it was the way to build products on the cheap. The problem of finding good people came up early and often at Board meetings and their response was predictable, *"How about India?"* However, I and my commiserating peers knew that it was nearly impossible to make those distant places work when it came to developing software products.

We also knew that it wasn't cheaper, either. Not when you took into account the unavoidable, long, and expensive trips in both directions. Not when you factored in all the rework that resulted from miscommunications and misunderstandings. Cultural differences and language barriers created all kinds of friction. Not being available to speak directly with each other was a killer.

You couldn't resolve even simple questions in real time. Instead, a string of emails would fly back and forth, each one getting longer than the previous. Frustration would build up at both ends and what started as a small, simple question would become a major complicated problem.

And then there was the high turnover. As more of us sent work overseas, demand grew beyond capacity and vendors were luring developers away from each other at a very high rate. This meant that a team never achieved a very good understanding of the product, leading to a lot of rework.

The need for finding an alternate source of developers was real. *And if we could find them nearby in Mexico...*

Opportunity Cost

The issue was not so much the money spent in salaries as it was the cost of lost opportunities. Whenever I found good local developers, money was no problem and we would pay whatever it took to get them to join.

The reason we tried so hard to make those remote places work was in the hope that we could find developers faster and grow our teams a little bit quicker. Otherwise, we could not keep up with customer demands and risked missing the opportunity.

DOT-COM (& DOT-GONE)

During the *dot-com* bubble[2] it became nearly impossible to find software developers or testers or anybody with product development experience. Investment capital was overabundant and lots of new software businesses were springing up very quickly. Developers were getting BMWs as sign-on bonuses! Then, the bubble burst: *"On March 10 [2000], the combined value of stocks on the NASDAQ was at $6.71 trillion... On April 6, 2000, it was $5.78 trillion. In less than a month, nearly a trillion dollars' worth of stock value had completely evaporated. ... companies were losing between $10 and $30 million a quarter."*[3]

Things cooled off after the bust and for a while it became a bit easier to find developers, but that didn't last long. The bust didn't stop software from *"eating the world"* as Marc Andreesen put it.[4] It barely slowed down its growth back then, and it has accelerated since.

Offshoring

Software outsourcing in the form of offshoring got big in the late 1990s because the year 2000 was going to be a big problem for many organizations. That's because in most cases the year had been saved as two digits instead of four. Storage was expensive back then and keeping half the digits made sense. For example, if your birth year was 1919, most software saved it as 19.

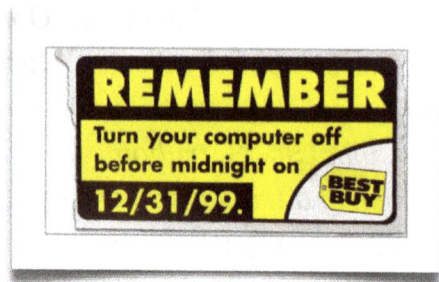

REMEMBER
Turn your computer off before midnight on 12/31/99.
BEST BUY

As the deadline approached, Western businesses rushed to fix the bug, popularly called *"the Y2K bug,"* that might bring down their digital systems and their businesses.[5] To do so, they ended up hiring lots of software people in India and in Eastern Europe.

India sounded ideal for that work, with lots of well-educated, English-speaking developers who were very inexpensive relative to the US and Europe. They would pore over their customers' code and find every instance of 19 and change it back to 1919. They also had to change any calculation that assumed two-digit years instead of four. By doing so, they would prevent all sorts of cataclysms that were predicted at the time.

Outsourcing morphed to offshoring and expanded from a maintenance function to other aspects of software development. Many big corporations offshored their whole IT operations to third parties in India and Eastern Europe. They saw their IT departments as a cost center and offshoring them,

- Made them less costly, and

- Turned them into a variable expense.

Then, in the early 2000s, even small software product businesses followed suit, with the full encouragement of their Boards, and they started to offshore their product development. By 2005, many people had tried it and a few were starting to get disappointed with the offshoring model, including me.

Cultural friction and big time zone separations were the main causes of failure.

It Has Legs

As it all came together for me "... *in Mexico*" became my working hypothesis. But I had a problem: other than the language, I knew very little about Mexico and what little I knew was all wrong. Luckily, somewhere along the way, I got connected with Roberto Martinez, a Mexican National and my future partner.

I bounced off a few of my peers and, like me, they were enthusiastic about the possibility of growing their team nearby, where they could talk to developers any time. And they were thrilled to avoid the cultural friction and the late night and early morning calls.

The idea had legs.

It would be a welcome service, the market was big, and it would grow as the software industry grew. But we had to differentiate Nearsoft from traditional body shops.

Nearsoft's culture turned out to be the feature that people found most memorable and remarkable. *Mexico* opened the door and our culture closed the deal.

Not My First Choice

When I met my future business partner, Roberto Martinez, his company was not my first choice to work with. There were several more mature Mexican businesses that, at the time, seemed to make more sense as partners. I had assumed that partnering with several companies would afford me a faster time to market. These other businesses were more established and already had the staff and the experience. Unfortunately, as I worked with them, they all washed out, except Roberto's *C Cube Technologies.*

I didn't think of *C Cube* as my first choice because I was seduced by the traditional marks of success that the other businesses offered. However, it didn't take long to realize that regardless of pedigree, Roberto and his team were a better match. The *C Cube* team was focused on software product development and didn't do anything else. They had worked with US businesses before. They had the right cadence. They were very responsive and transparent. And they were committed to long term relationships, not hit-and-run jobs.

For example, one of the projects we worked on together ran late. I had committed to a fixed price, but I didn't manage it well and the project kept dragging. I ended up paying *C Cube* out of my own pocket and it was getting expensive. I spoke with Roberto and his partner Julio Gonzalez about it and without missing a beat they said something like, *"We are going to make the client happy, don't worry."*

The engineer who worked on the project, Rodrigo Yáñez, is brilliant. His design anticipated changes that the client later asked for. We ended up not making a profit, but the client was very happy with the result. It was a good reference for us afterwards.

Time Zones

At the time we started Nearsoft, software outsourcing and offshoring were completely conflated. The businesses in the US wanted to get more for less and offshoring offered to hire developers overseas for cheap and assign them the easy to do but mind-numbing work.

Offshoring had worked to correct the Y2K problem. And if it worked for that particular software problem, the thinking went, then it would work for any software development. But that particular fantasy didn't really work for product development.

Product development is not at all a rinse-and-repeat process. Successful products come from constant experimentation and close interaction with end users to figure out what they consider valuable. It is *impossible* to write a precise spec for the work to be done.

Everybody on the team, including developers, testers, and the product folks, need to talk with one another as problems and opportunities arise. And to do this effectively they have to be in sync, otherwise differences in the circadian cycle mess everything up.

I learned this tidbit at Sun Microsystems, when I was the boss of a group split between Mountain View, California, and Morrisville, North Carolina.[6] The two locations were *only* three time zones apart, but that was enough to throw us out of whack. By the time that the team in California was rolling in, the folks in North Carolina were on their way to lunch. Then, when the New Carolina folks were ready to get into their afternoon groove, the folks in California were heading out for lunch. I took that lesson with me.

When we started Nearsoft we only pursued clients that were within one or two time zones of our office in Hermosillo,   the capital of Sonora, Mexico.

Responsibility vs Authority

Before Sun Microsystems I had worked mostly in smallish startups where taking the initiative was valued and encouraged.

When I first joined, Sun was still at the stage that taking the initiative was valued. Nine years later, Sun had more than 10,000 people[7] and the culture had definitely taken a turn towards the corporate, bureaucratic way.

Most of my time at Sun was in the Graphics & Multimedia side of the house, first in hardware and later in software. We were the supporting cast; the main attraction was the workstation and server folks on the hardware side, and the Operating System folks on the software side. I didn't realize it then, but the supporting cast was a great place to be. We knew our customers, kept them happy, and were free to take the initiative and make decisions big and small along the way. We had responsibility *and* authority (*i.e.*, 'we' the bosses, of course).

Then I was made a bigger boss in charge of the Operating Systems team. I had been entrusted with Solaris, the company's crown jewels! It was my reward for taking initiative, I thought. But the increase in responsibility came with a decrease in authority. Because it was so central to the rest of Sun's products, everybody wanted to weigh in on every decision related to Solaris. Decisions that would have gone unnoticed in the Graphics & Multimedia side of the house, now became objects of universal concern, scrutinized by all, critiqued, and questioned. And often reversed by my bosses.

For example, one of the perennial problems with Solaris was that releases were always late. Every new piece of hardware, every new networking feature, every software library had to go out together on the same *release train*. As the train got bigger, the release dates became more and more unpredictable. Departure time was anybody's guess.

There were precious few rules for getting on the train. And what few rules we had were often gamed or outright broken. So we tried to streamline the rules and make them stick.

Very often, new code would *break the build.* That is what we called it when new software was added and it stopped Solaris from working. When this happened, no new code could be added until the faulty code was fixed. We wanted to change this, so we decided that the next time new code broke the build, we would take it out and move it to the end of the line waiting to get on the train. If it was fixed before the train left the station, great, but otherwise, the software train would ship on time. But, hey, the fixed code would be at the head of the line for the next train.[8]

What we had come up with would make releases predictable. But as it turned out, I didn't have the authority to take this kind of initiative. People who had been through this before warned me. The call from Sun's CEO, Scott McNealy, didn't take long,

McNealy	Is it true that you told your people to take {CODENAME} out of the release?
Matt	Yes, it…
McNealy	Put it back in the release.
Matt	But their code breaks the build and…

McNealy	Put it back in the release. Got that?
Matt	OK, but it just doesn't wor…
McNealy	>click<

I talked to the people who had warned me and told them about the call. They were disappointed by the news, but not surprised. They completed my schooling by letting me know that this also meant that we would have to fix the code ourselves. Solaris had to support the featured hardware as it had already been announced.

I lasted less than two years as the Solaris kinda boss.

I know this situation doesn't sound pretty, but I don't mean it as a criticism of Sun and how it was run back then. None of us knew any different. More than anything, I want to illustrate how in spite of being very innovative in technology, Sun could not innovate itself out of the Fiat hierarchy that eventually smothered it. If anything, it continued to *go corporate* and eventually faded away.

The lesson I took away from this is that responsibility and authority are essential, not only for working effectively with others, but for the personal feeling of satisfaction. Being responsible for software delivery but having little authority to make changes left me very frustrated.

That gave me an inkling of what others must have felt like when I, unilaterally, snatched away their ability to act independently.

The Most Important Lesson

Climbing the ladder of Fiat success at Sun and elsewhere did not come for free. My family, too, paid the price of all the so-called success. I had climbed up the proverbial ladder, grabbed power whenever I had the chance, and wielded the double-edged sword of fear. All while navigating the corporate moral maze and the ethical traps along the way. I could not help but bring a lot of these habits and stress home with me every night.

In *Rehumanizing the Workplace*, Chuck Blakeman points out that "... *management is...*

unadulterated codependence... Managers are enablers." [9] At home I was the enabler dad, much like I behaved at work. I was inflexible (*"because I said so"*), wanted my children to meet my needs (*"you're gonna be great at... "*), and wanted to solve problems for them (*"you should have punched him back harder!"*). We survived it, but not without pain.

I don't wish this kind of pain on anybody, or their families.

A Different Approach to Management

Anyone who has started a company knows that it's critical for the founders to be aligned when it comes to priorities and values. When Roberto and I talked about merging our companies, he said, *"I want to build a company that works for everyone."* That simple notion—that everyone should enjoy their work and share in the wealth—was at the foundation of the company. We were also in lockstep on a long list of things we didn't want at Nearsoft – we didn't want to be bosses, we didn't want *employees*, we didn't want titles, we didn't want to hide information about the company, and so on.

It all took time to evolve, learning many lessons along the way. But, strange as it sounds, it took a crisis to convince us that we were on our way.

Near-Death Experience

The Nearsoft story almost came to an end after barely getting off the ground. In hindsight, this near-death experience was the best thing to happen to us because it showed us that we could manage the company without bosses.

In 2009 the financial crisis hit us.[10] Several of our clients folded, some reduced the size of their teams, and others stopped spending on anything but the bare necessities.

We tried all kinds of things, but by mid-year it was pretty clear that we had to roll back our expenses or else. Ironically, Roberto and I had just started to pay ourselves a steady salary and Nearsoft had moved into new offices, with room to grow.

Here to Stay

We were faced with the prospect of laying people off. The reasonable thing to do would have been for Roberto and myself to draw a list of people to lay off and that would have been it. I don't think people would have questioned it back then. They would not be surprised that we, as owners, did this. In fact, they might have excused it (*"they did their best... they had to do it..."*).

But we would have known that it wasn't our best. I know that Roberto and I would have felt terrible and lost sleep over it for a long time.

Instead, we did the most democratic thing we could think of at the time: we put it to a vote. (That ended up being the only time we've voted on anything, having since realized that voting is a pretty ham-fisted way of making decisions).

Rejected

After telling people what was happening and sharing the details of where we were financially, we suggested that we all take a small percentage cut in salary. That would allow us to keep going through the end of the year when, we hoped, things would change for the better.

We voted, ... and the proposal was rejected.

We were disappointed and we were strongly tempted to just do it all ourselves at that point, but we didn't. The Force[11] held strong.

After we cooled off, we could see that taking a pay cut didn't make sense to most people. For one, we had not yet formalized a stock option plan, so nobody else even had a financial stake in the company. Sure, they would be preserving their jobs, but they all could get new jobs easily.

They would be leaving behind a workspace where we treated each other as adults and instead go back to having to *pretty please* the boss for everything. But at that point, co-management at Nearsoft was new and untested. Maybe the naysayers were right and it would eventually fade away.

There was the very real likelihood that come the end of the year, we might have to close down the company anyway. And in the meantime, the nail-biting would be intense.

So, we tried a different approach.

We decided to form a committee to decide who was in and who was out. Several people were voted onto this committee. Roberto and I deliberately stayed out of this process.

After a couple of days, the committee was done and we did as they had decided. It was painful, but to my surprise, it was not demoralizing.

Being part of the process, however imperfect, meant that there were no surprises. There was no hand wringing over whether or not it was fair. There was no second-guessing why certain people had been let go and not others. The folks who sat on the committee could, and did, explain their choices, one peer to another.

It had been scary and messy, but it also made it clear that our fledgling co-management at Nearsoft was here to stay. If we could deal with this very difficult decision as a team, then we could manage the company as a team. We had to figure out how to do it, but that, we hoped, would be the fun part.

Inspired by Maverick

About a year after the founding of Nearsoft, one of the co-authors, Adrian Perez, discovered a book called *Maverick*[12] and he insisted that I read it. About a few pages into the book, I excitedly badgered Roberto to read it.

Maverick is a book about a Brazilian manufacturer which Ricardo Semler, its author, inherited from his father. He tried to manage things his dad's way, but that didn't go well. After suffering a nervous breakdown, Semler decided to remake the company, to make it truly people centric in a non-patriarchal way. This meant things like letting people decide their own hours of operation, having workers sit on Board meetings, and opening the books and training people to make sense of them.

It was a head-exploding moment for us. Somebody had done it before. It showed us a path. And it helped put co-management at Nearsoft on a firmer footing. Other early books that have been very influential in our journey were *Tribal Leadership*,[13] *PEAK*,[14] and *The Dream Manager*.[15]

From the very start, we wanted to create a place where people could be themselves, enjoy each other, and contribute in unexpected, innovative ways. From personal experience, I knew that traditional management was painful and dehumanizing for all involved, bosses and workers alike—Roberto and I didn't want any of that. Semler's Maverick helped us see that we were not crazy or naïve for wanting something different.

Maverick showed us that we could shape a different future for all of us at Nearsoft. Most of all, it made it clear that co-management wasn't just the absence of titles, corner offices, and managers. It required the development of a whole new organizational structure and practices.

It sounded like a lot of work, and it has been. And it's been worth it every step of the way. It allowed Nearsoft to thrive, not just survive. We made a bunch of mistakes along the way, but we also learned from them.

We also got some very big things right, including our approach to decentralized decision making, which we call Leadership Teams, and the way we distribute dividends.

Leadership Teams

A Leadership Teams is a light-weight mechanism for decentralized decision making. They are a key practice at Nearsoft.

The word *leadership* is somewhat confusing for new people and they assume that it has to do with Roberto and me. They don't immediately recognize that *they* are the leaders and *they* are the ones who bring people together in a Leadership Team, at any time, for any purpose.

The only rule is that the Team be transparent and publish their minutes and conclusions. People who are going to be impacted by the decision must be involved in shaping it. There is no requirement to have one person speak at a time, or hold a symbolic stick, or any other procedure like that, although a Leadership Team may use these and other practices, if appropriate.

What involved means depends on the situation, but in general it includes no surprises. It may include a consultation step, a bit reminiscent of the Advice Process,[16] a term coined by Dennis Bakke at AES Corp to refer to the concept of *"empowering team members who identify a problem or opportunity to take the initiative to address the situation."* In our case, we don't empower anybody—we all come with all the power we need. And since there are no bosses at Nearsoft, there's no requirement to *"ask your boss"* as there is with the Advice Process.

Leadership Teams tackle all types of decisions at Nearsoft and have been remarkably effective in terms of engaging people in the process, resulting in better decisions. *"Nothing about us without us."*[17]

Earned Dividends

From the very start, we shared the company's Dividends at Nearsoft. Roberto developed a distribution formula which worked for us for a while.

Roberto's formula got very sophisticated, so much so that most people didn't understand it. But we all trusted Roberto and we knew that it must be fair. As we kept growing, the formula got even more inscrutable and in 2014, a small group of people decided to change it. They formed a Leadership Team and went about revising the Earned Dividends formula.

A Nearsoftian, Luis Galaz, brought together a Leadership Team and they went to work on the Earned Dividend formula. They tried out different ideas and consulted with lots of people and in general they treated the decision as what leadership author and consultant David Marquet calls a below-the-waterline[18] decision, a decision critical to the health of the company.

When they finally came out with a new formula, it was very simple: in the future, the end-of-year distribution would be calculated by dividing the total Earned Dividends by the number of Nearsoftians. That was it. Everyone would get an equal part of it. And that meant everybody, from the people responsible for cleaning to Roberto and me.

Not everybody thought it was a good idea. *"It ignores my contribution! And what about all the years I spent going to school?"* There were lots of questions, but no significant push back. There was *consent* as Sociocracy practitioners would call it, so we decided to try it for a couple of years. *"If it doesn't work, you can form another Leadership Team that incorporates whatever we learned from the experience."*

I were among the people who didn't quite like it and I was fully expecting that it would not last. Then, one day in the Hermosillo kitchen, I heard a new Nearsoftian call it *simplistic.* The answer, from the Nearsoftian he was talking to was powerful: *"Look, we did as well as we did because of everybody, right? Trying to split hairs about specific contributions would be counter-productive, don't you think? And who would be the judge of that?"*

That made sense to me.

As much as anything else, this formula was easy to understand and there was no wizard behind the curtain deciding how to split the wealth we all worked for. You could *trust it*.

In the words of Nobel Prize winner Elinor Ostrom, *"Right at the center of trying to understand how people solve dilemmas is the challenge of their developing trust in one another."*[19] Trust removes many of the worries that otherwise can sap people's energy. A more complicated formula may be technically more complete, but it's not necessarily better. On the other hand, an easy-to-understand formula can be trusted and not have to worry that they are being suckered.

It's worth noting that an equitable distribution is the goal, not equality. We'll say more about this in the second part of this book.

Totally Nuts

When we told people outside the company about our wealth sharing, they think we are nuts. Nearsoft had no outside investors or shareholders, so part of the profits are distributed as Earned Dividends among all

Nearsoftians, another part is reserved for the following year. As a friend told me, this practice was "*naïve and totally nuts and it will never work.*" But it did.

How to Not Motivate People

It's important to note that at Nearsoft, we don't use Earned Dividends as a form of 'motivation.'

Motivation comes from inside each of us. Outside of work people readily self-direct and do what they have to do to meet their commitments.

Profit Sharing programs, as they are popularly known, usually try to reward things like,

- Individual accomplishments

- Individual expertise

- Individual academic degrees and other accreditations

- Individual contributions to the company's financial performance

- Whatever management wants.

Straight from *Theory X*,[20] the presumption is that all it takes is cash to motivate all those "*indolent and irresponsible*" people. But a once-a-year bump in income does nothing to promote any changes the following year. "*A satisfied need (for money) no longer motivates.*"[21] Once they get their annual bonus, people go back to doing what's expected of them. As a means of, "*motivating them, controlling their actions, modifying their behavior to fit the needs of the organization.*"[22] The annual bonus doesn't work as intended.

Freeloading

A question that comes up regularly is about freeloading. How do you prevent people from taking advantage of it all? The short answer is that freeloading does not happen in co-managed companies like Nearsoft.

Freeloading happens in the Fiat context because,

- Freeloading is considered a sin or a disease
- The boss has to catch the freeloader in the act

- The freeloader's co-workers don't care to report it when they see it.

At Nearsoft, we have not experienced freeloading as such. In the few cases where people were not delivering on what they've promised, or repeatedly gave *the dog ate my homework* kind of excuses. But there was something else going on that led to that behavior. It was not laziness or evil intent or a case of stealing from thy neighbor. Freeloading is usually a symptom, not the disease.

In one case it turned out that the *freeloader* was so used to being told what to do that when nobody said anything, he just didn't do anything. This happened in the very early days of Nearsoft. In all other cases, it turned out to be a side-effect of depression, something happening at home, or something along those lines. In one case it was about self-medicating that got out of hand and led to addiction.

In each case, Nearsoftians dealt with it according to its circumstances. In one case, we had to let one person go; in other cases, Nearsoftians managed to get people the help they needed to deal with their personal situations. In the addiction case, Nearsoftians got his family involved, they got him back to health, and he continues to be a healthy Nearsoftian to this day.

Good News!

Nearsoft was acquired in 2017. Roberto and I had not planned on selling Nearsoft, but in 2015, the economic and political picture in the US (Trump) and Mexico (Lopez Obrador) started to look unstable and we were getting a bit nervous.

In any case, even though we were not looking for a buyer, a buyer found us.

It sounds weird now, but at the time, we didn't even think of involving anybody else in the decision. We just didn't think of it at the time. In fact, the concept of co-ownership didn't come into focus for me until *way after* the acquisition.

It's Official

In 2015 Nearsoft had been successfully acquired! All Nearsoftians owned a piece of the company and benefited financially from the sale. The effort had worked for everyone.

The new owners recognized the value of the co-managed culture that had developed at Nearsoft. They liked our level of engagement and appreciated *the energy* they sensed at Nearsoft.

It was time to celebrate.

We knew that we would have to explain what it meant to each and every one of us. Being a shareholder had not meant much to most Nearsoftians up to this point. Holding a piece of paper that said *"you own ye-many shares"* had very little context in Mexico, even in the technology sector.

We knew that adults don't like surprises and people would be concerned, but this one was unavoidable. At one point during these talks we signed a Nondisclosure Agreement and had to keep the whole process under wraps. Now that it was done the questions gushed out: *"How is this going to impact me?"* *"Am I going to lose my job?"* *"Will it change Nearsoft's culture?"*

The easiest thing to explain was what it meant financially. Most Nearsoftians owned a piece of the company and they would benefit directly from the acquisition. Even the newbies benefited because those of us who had shares were taken off the Earned Dividend pool and the newbies got the whole pool for themselves (*i.e.*, the numerator stayed the same while the denominator got a lot smaller).

Roberto had warned me that people were going to be very surprised, even shocked. I nodded my head in agreement then, but it didn't quite sink in. After more than 30 years in technology in Silicon Valley, *exits* were old hat for me. Not so for the other Nearsoftians. As the actual checks started to come in, people were still a bit incredulous. *"Can I take my kids to Disneyland?" "Can I buy a house?"*

The concerns that came up later took longer to deal with.

Great, But...

The most common questions were about the future of Nearsoft and our distinct culture. Nearsoftians valued it, dearly, and the acquisition could be a threat to it. *"Would we get managers now?" "Would the new owners change how we do things?"*

As fear crept up on people, all kinds of rumors arose about what might be coming. Luckily, people were used to speaking up.

For us, that's one of the many values of co-management: learning to be responsible for your concerns, voicing them, and resolving them collaboratively. A rumor would come up, somebody would bring it out in the open, and the answers would be discussed, digested, and disseminated throughout Nearsoft. After about a month or so, things settled down.

A Lot Left to Be Done

The acquisition was more evidence that co-management not only worked, but it worked better than Fiat management. The money that would have gone to bosses, we spent it on ourselves instead and still managed to generate a very healthy margin.

We hold two Team Building Weeks every year where all Nearsoftians come to work together in one place. Clients join us, too. In Spring, we usually go to a nice place, like Cancún, or a place of historical significance, like Querétaro. The Winter Team Building

Week is capped off with a grand end-of-year party. We can afford to do things like this because we don't waste money on bosses and the illusion of control.

By the way, these Team Building events weren't always a hit, but they are an example of what happens when the organizers and the participants are the same people. The feedback we got from the first couple of events was pretty negative. *"Why do I have to waste time playing these stupid games," "The speaker didn't know anything about us," "We paid for that bullshit?"* But because the organizers were also participants, they kept making them more useful over time by simply doing less of what sucked and more of what worked.

People have blossomed into the leaders they didn't think they could be. Introverts with quiet voices have led the creation of events of all sizes, like NearsoftCon, a full-blown event with external speakers and all the rest of it. We've seen people grow in ways that would have been impossible in the shadow of a Fiat hierarchy. I like to think that their growth has benefited their families and communities, too.

Regardless of all the good stuff, there's a lot more to be done, particularly, in the area of ownership. Self-management is becoming more popular and all, but it is not enough.

Co-Management Is Not Enough

My own questions started to bubble up a couple of years after the acquisition. I felt good about it and the team we had joined—that was not the issue. We had moved to a bigger stage, from a regional player to a global one. It also gave us a chance to learn and that was good.

Regardless, I had the sense that there was work left to be done. Yes, we had all benefited financially, but most of us had not learned to be owners, at least not fully, even though we had haphazardly taken a step in that direction. But there was so much more that we hadn't explored.

Capital Allocation

Each year, Roberto and I decided how much of our profits to use as capital for the following year and how much to leave in the Dividend pool. It just never occurred to us to include others in this decision. If we had thought of it, we would probably have dismissed the idea right off. *"They don't understand Nearsoft's financial situation, so why put this on them?"*

We decided how to divide the pie and the size of the employee pool. We chose how to allocate the shares in that pool and decided how many shares each cohort would get. All very reasonable and fair. We were the owners, so we made the call. But in doing so, what issues were we blind to? What opportunities had we missed? These and similar questions were bouncing around in my head.

After a while it all started to come together for me: co-management was not enough! We needed a model of ownership that went beyond not having bosses. A model that formally decentralized ownership distribution, capital allocation, and all other aspects of being an owner. And we needed to figure out how to get everybody involved in dealing with these issues.

The Fiat Apocalypse

Unhappy at Work

You've probably seen the claim that *"people are unhappy at work."* It's all over the Web in blogs, videos, surveys, and academic papers. It is very dramatic, makes good headlines, and it is also very true.

According to one of their reports, "The global aggregate from Gallup data collected in 2014, 2015 and 2016 across 155 countries indicates that just 15% of employees worldwide are engaged in their job. Two-thirds are not engaged and 18% are actively disengaged."[23] To be clear, "actively disengaged" means that more than unhappy people are numb.

You may not be all that unhappy, not in general. At least, not all the time. You like the people you work with, most of them, in any case. And the work itself is not quite bad. It's just that things could be better.

I've been extremely lucky. I really enjoy what I do and the people I do it with. At our company we make up its rules and policies and when they no longer work, we change them. Some, like Paul Buchheit[24] are even luckier. He is the creator of Gmail and has worked at Sun Microsystems and Facebook and ended up a very wealthy person. In his words,

I don't have to work. I choose to work. And I believe everyone deserves the same freedom I have. If done right, it's also economically superior, meaning we will all have more wealth. We often talk about how brilliant or visionary Steve Jobs was, but there are probably millions of people just as brilliant as he was. The difference is they likely didn't grow up with great parents, amazing teachers, and an environment where innovation was the norm. Also they didn't live down the street from Steve Wozniak.

> Economically, we don't need more jobs. We need more Steve Jobs. ... When we set everyone free, we enable the outliers everywhere. The result will be an unprecedented boom in human creativity and ingenuity.

More co-owners, more Steve Jobs. More people would be more engaged and fully alive. Or as economist Umai Haque put it we'd be *"rich with relationships, ideas, emotion, health and vigor, recognition and contribution, passion and fulfillment, and great accomplishment and enduring achievement."*[25]

I have a hunch that our economy would also grow healthier, more just, and financially stronger.

The Other Huge Problem

The other huge problem is Capitalism, as currently practiced.

Once upon a time, to me, Capitalism was the opposite of Communism. Communism was Fidel Castro's dictatorship in Cuba, where I was born and raised, and Capitalism was the US Declaration of Independence and Benjamin Franklin. At the age of 14, we were lucky enough and my family got me out to Spain. At the time, Spain was less dysfunctional than Cuba's, but it was a dictatorship, nevertheless. It started to look like things were not as simple as I had once thought.

These days I recognize that what we call Capitalism hurts the overwhelming majority of us. It even hurts those who benefit most from it financially, although they don't talk about it with the exception of Warren Buffet and precious few others, such as billionaire Ray Dalio.[26] In 2019 he stated, *"Capitalism basically is not working for the majority of people."*

I am not aching for a revolution. Revolutions just bring in a different set of bosses without changing the structure itself for the better. More generally, we are not thinking of government as the solution. Rather than relying on policies and taxes to fix it, people can transform the system from the ground up and from the inside out. This can happen without doing away with the good aspects of capital. If we transform ownership, then Capitalism will change along with it. In the Radical paradigm, ownership remains private but it is much broader and dynamic than today.

Fiat Businesses

The big obstacle to this transformation is our current concept of ownership. *"This is my business, I make the decisions, not you."* This assumption is invisible, taken for granted.

Visibility!

We don't even have a term for all the forms of private ownership. We have sole ownerships, partnerships, and various forms of corporations. We could not find a term for all of them as a class, so we called them Fiat businesses. Run as dictatorships and owned like feudal estates.

At the top of the hierarchy is the Board of Directors, and below them are the Executives. Below them are lesser bosses, and ever lesser bosses below them. At the very bottom is everybody else. Altogether they make up what we call a Fiat hierarchy,

Imposed Hierarchies
with Boss on Top

FIAT HIERARCHY   ALSO FIAT HIERARCHY

The Fiat Hierarchy

This hierarchy is all about executing the will of the Fiat owners, the Board. These owners control all the wealth the business creates. According to current law they are fiducially responsible to act in the interest of shareholders, which has come to mean that they have to make sure the business creates capital. Everything else is secondary, at best. *"What's good for the business is good for the workers."*[27]

We might have gotten rid of the divine right of kings and queens, but we didn't do anything about the divine right of capital. We left the corporate aristocracy in control of the wealth.

Behind the front door of every Fiat business, the owners still rule as kings and queens.

Feudal Estates

Most businesses today are run like feudal estates. The owners are entitled to make decisions, regardless of the impact to employees. Only the Fiat owners have the authority to decide on matters of ownership,

- Who gets how many shares?

- How much in retained earnings?

- How much to keep for themselves?

- How much to distribute as bonuses?

Employees don't get to participate in making any of these decisions. And the same goes for common shareholders who don't have a say in any of this, either.

Ready for War

War Machines

Businesses are envisioned as war machines. Today's businesses are rife with war terms and metaphors. Battle-tested, rally the troops, capture a market, dominate a segment. We've ended up with a militarized economy that takes a toll on everybody's wellbeing.

Enough!

We need to step away from this *"economy that is dependent on perpetual war"*[28] before it obliterates us. We need a different enough paradigm that is sustainable in the long-term. We need an economy that won't crush us under its weight. Or as Mark Carney, governor of the Bank of England said in 2020, we need *"... a fit planet for our grandchildren to live on."*[29] Businesses don't have to be ready for war at all times. Even if they were in a battle with live bullets, they don't need to be at war at all times.

Pirates knew that.

Pirates and Democracy

In the pirate ships of yore *"Captains retained absolute authority in times of battle."*[30] The rest of the time, the navigator could argue with the Captain all day long, and sailors could vote for a destination other than the one favored by the Captain. But during battle, do as the Captain says (or else). This was one of the things spelled out in a constitutional document that real pirates operated by.

These constitutions even spelled out how much of the loot each sailor would get. Generally, sailors would get one unit of the loot, the Quartermaster one and half, and the Captain two units. When it's all said and done, pirates were a pretty Radical bunch.

CEOs are often called *"Captain of the ship."* This is problematic in many ways, not the least of which is that this means Fiat businesses are engaged in a perpetual war. Through that looking glass, all they see is enemies. The cost of employees, customer support, supplier pricing: they are all enemies clawing away at my loot... er... profits. We talk with pride about capturing customers and locking them in. Crushing the competition. Putting golden handcuffs on the best employees. Locking them up with sign-on bonuses that they'd have to pay back if they leave.

This is pathological, at best. It's not surprising that people feel tense, bosses and employees alike. If, as a boss, you view yourself as a battle Captain, then you'll expect people to jump overboard at your say so, of course. As a boss, the frustration you feel when people don't immediately do as you say arises from that expectation. I've felt this frustration myself.

As an employee you are always in battle mode, too. You get good at following the Captain's command, or at least pretending to do so. Don't speak up, don't argue, just say *ay-ay, sir* (and be ready to blame it on somebody else if it doesn't work).

People have internalized this constant state of battle; the boss has embraced the Captain persona and employees have learned to salute without a second thought. No wonder people feel stressed at work: they spend their days in a war zone.

A Peacetime Company

We wondered why there hasn't been a move to 'stand down' over time, away from the perpetual war position. After a horrific conflagration like WWII, why didn't we get wise to the need for a different approach? Particularly, given the post-WWII economic expansion[31] and the sustained period of growth and prosperity that followed, why didn't we adopt more of a peacetime model for our businesses and our economy?

Ernst Bader got an inkling of this war stance and wanted to move his company away from it. Bader had founded the Scott Bader company in 1921. In 1951, right after WWII, Bader and his family turned 90% of their shares to a Trust and all the company's dividends to its *members* (*i.e.,* that's what he called them to differentiate them from *employees*). He wanted to promote "*an alternative to a war-based capitalist economy.*"[32]

A few years later W L Gore and Associates took the peacetime path from the start. In 1958, Bill and Genevieve Gore founded their company in their basement.[33] From the start, the company didn't have bosses or assigned teams. They were aware of the scaling issue built into traditional hierarchies and of how bureaucracy takes over as companies get bigger. As author Bernard Schroeder writes, "... *Bill Gore felt that when a unit of workers got big enough, it actually began to fall apart. Gore understood that workers in a 150-person unit could all know one another and share a commitment to group goals and values and that any growth beyond that would change those dynamics.*"[34] The 150-person number is now known as the Dunbar number, but Bill Gore came to it by trial and error.[35]

In the long run, it has worked out really well for them. "*Gore has grown revenues to nearly $3 billion and consistently turned a profit since its founding in 1958. It has approximately 9000 employees at 30 locations worldwide.*"[36] As of this writing, the company generates $3.7 billion in annual revenues and over 10,500 associates worldwide who are also co-owners of the company.

W L Gore & Associates has accomplished this without an all-powerful battle Captain at the helm. It is the closest example of a co-managed and co-owned company that we know of and it is fantastically successful and inspirational.

The Ownership Puzzle

At the funeral of Eduard VII, *Britain, 1910*.
Standing: Haakon VII, *Norway*; Ferdinand I, *Bulgaria*; Manuel II, *Portugal*; Guillaume (Wilhelm) II, *Germany*; George(s) I, *Roi des Hellènes*; Albert I, *Belgium*.
Sitting: Alfonso XIII, Spain; George V, Britain; Frédéric VIII, Denmark.

A Society of Kings

In 1776, the US declared that the people could govern ourselves better than King George III could. He was no longer the owner of everything and citizens would be the owners instead. Decentralized property was the key to our liberty.

But this new form of government, a republican democracy, was going to be run by property owners, freeholders, men of leisure. People who had *"time given to study and becoming enlightened about universal truths and appropriate governmental policies."*[37]

Unfortunately, this narrowed considerably who had the right to vote. By design, it excluded women, Native Americans, and most definitely the enslaved[38] who were the property that made up a significant part of the wealth of said citizens. It also excluded from voting anybody who had to labor for a living, namely poor Europeans people. Laborers were financially dependent on the owner class and were not considered free enough to vote.

The new system decentralized ownership, but in a very limited way. Nevertheless, it enshrined private property as the basis of liberty: the power that previously had been reserved for King George III was now in the hands of owners of land and people.

1792 Profit-Sharing

The founders did know about co-ownership and were aware of its virtues. As Dr Joseph Blasi points that out in *A Founding Father Profit Sharing Fix for Inequality*,

On February 16, 1792, Washington signed into law a bill from the U.S. Congress that cut taxes for ship owners and sailors in the American cod fishery, in an effort to revive the failing industry. However, the tax cut was conditioned on *a broad-based profit-sharing arrangement between shipowners and the crews—a centuries-long custom of sharing the profits made from every catch.* The legislation was supported by two politicians who typically agreed on very little: Secretary of the Treasury Alexander Hamilton and Secretary of State Thomas Jefferson... *ships with profit-sharing were more productive than those with fixed wages.*[39] (emphasis added)

In any case, it would be unfair and more than a little arrogant to rain on the founders' parade from today's perspective. What they did was very revolutionary at the time. The Declaration of Independence is aspirational and brilliant for its time. The economic system that emerged has brought us a lot of material good, but it has also caused a lot of misery. And, as it is, the system is fast approaching an ugly dead end, but we must not submit to this fate.

We will find ways to preserve our common good, our commonwealth. Management author and venerated guru, Peter Drucker believed that businesses could be a force for good, but he assumed that only bosses could do it: "*If the managers of our major institutions, and especially of business, do not take responsibility for the common good, no one else can or will.*"[40] Well, nearly 50 years have passed since Drucker wrote this and the bosses have not taken "*responsibility for the common good.*" In fact, they have abused it. Wish as we will, bosses will not be the agents of benevolent change that Drucker imagined.

Although he was wrong about the bosses, Drucker was right, in our opinion, in implying that businesses could be effective agents of change. As Kim Jordan, co-founder of New Belgium Brewing, put it, *"Business is a powerful tool in making the kind of world that we want to live in."*[41]

Everything that developed at New Belgium over the years was Radical: the use of Open Book Management, an ESOP (Employee Stock Ownership Plan)[44] through which its workers eventually owned 100%[42] of the company, and the involvement of everybody in planning and managing the company. Everybody at New Belgium felt like owners because they were the real owners, not symbolic owners. One of them exclaimed that he could deal with the complex paperwork and negotiations of buying a house, *"because I'm an owner in New Belgium, and there's Open-Book Management, then I'm able to do this $500,000 transaction. A warehouse worker, a forklift driver is doing this."*[43]

Karl Marx

Karl Marx tried his hand at the ownership issue. Unfortunately, his formulation took for granted the same Fiat hierarchy paradigm: there's gotta be a boss, so the proletariat shall be the boss. Instead of having all the wealth concentrated in the hands of Fiat owners, put it in the hands of the proletariat, the people who produced the wealth in the first place.

Inspired by Marx, the Bolsheviks rallied behind Lenin to instantiate this ideal in 1917.[44] Unfortunately, since Marx hadn't really figured out how to implement the proletariat-as-boss concept, it fell to the Bolshevik dictatorship to play the role of the all-powerful, universal boss. On behalf of the proletariat, of course.

Spoiler alert: it didn't work well for anybody, particularly the proletariat.

Henry George

In 1879 Henry George,[45] an American economist, published *Progress and Poverty*.[46] The book became really popular and by the 1890s: it was second only to the Christian Bible in the number of copies sold in the US. It also caught on throughout the world and even inspired San Yat-sen, *"one of the greatest leaders of modern China."*[47]

Land Rent Goes to Society

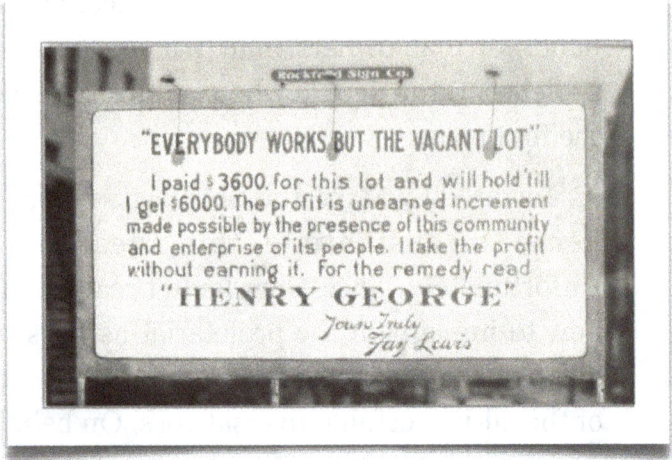

EVERYBODY WORKS BE THE VACAN LOT
I paid $3600 for this lot and will hold 'till I get $6000. The profit is unearned increment made possible by the presence of this community and enterprise of its people. I take the profit without earning it. For the remedy read "HENRY GEORGE"

— Yours Truly, Fay Lewis.

According to George, rent from land should accrue to society, not to landowners. In other words, land and its surrounding community should not be treated as income but as capital. A vacant lot in a growing neighborhood would grow up in value by virtue of the improvements around it. As others build houses, businesses, and parks nearby, the value of the vacant lot goes up.

It follows then that the new, higher rent should go to the community who raised the value of the land, not the landowner who did nothing for it. George noted that *"nothing that is freely supplied by nature can be properly classed as capital."*[48]

Landowners would keep the rights to profit for any improvements, but not the rent for the land itself. People could farm it or build houses on it and the results of their work and investment would still belong to them. But the rent from the land itself belongs to society. As professor Dr Francis Peddle put it, *"The return to land (nature) ought to be appropriated by society."*[49]

George's proposal featured a land tax as a way for society to recover the rent that the landowner was not entitled to. As much as anything else, this made the proposal an easy target for those opposed to it. Even many years later, well-known economist Milton Friedman could only bring himself to call it, *"the least bad tax."*[50]

From my own experience, our house has gone up nearly 10 times in value since we bought it in 1984. We have kept it up, but nothing that would justify such a rise. The upsurge in value comes mostly from the beautiful houses that sprung up around us, the ever-growing technology business in the area, excellent schools, and the infrastructure that holds it together.

Monopoly

I first heard about George in the context of the game of Monopoly. The game was invented by Elizabeth Phillips (neé Magie)[51] and originally had two sets of rules.[52] In the *monopolist* version, called The Landlord's Game, players would buy property and charge rent to other players; a player wins when all others go broke. Those are the rules that survive as today's Monopoly game.

The anti-monopolist version, called Prosperity, showed how George's proposals would deal with the problems that traditional ownership of land created. In this version of the game, players would benefit through a single tax on land. With this tax the community would buy private services (*e.g.*, commuter train services) and make them free to all players. The landowners could keep the wealth created by their labor and capital investments, untaxed.

Broad Impact

Henry George and his single land tax idea inspired a multitude of people. For example, his words had an indelible effect on George Bernard Shaw, "*I went one night, quite casually, into a hall in London, and I heard a man deliver a speech which changed the whole current of my life. That man was an American, Henry George.*"[53]

Hellen Keller waxed poetic about George's philosophy, "*I know I shall find in Henry George's philosophy a rare beauty and power of inspiration and a splendid faith in the essential nobility of human nature.*"[54]

Even Albert Einstein was enthusiastic about it, "*Men like Henry George are rare unfortunately. One cannot imagine a more beautiful combination of intellectual keenness, artistic form, and fervent love of justice. Every line is written as if for our generation.*"[55]

George's proposal is said to also have influenced many of the New Deal initiatives.[56]

However, in spite of all the enthusiasm it generated, replacing all taxes with a single land tax never came to pass, except fleetingly. His ideas were "*adopted to some degree in Australia, Hong Kong, Singapore, South Africa, South Korea, and Taiwan...*"[57] More recently the town of Altoona, Pennsylvania, temporarily implemented it, "*... phasing in the tax in 2002, relying on it entirely for tax revenue from 2011, and ending it 2017.*"[58]

Fear, Uncertainty, and Doubt

Reading George's master opus raised a question: it was such a straightforward idea and backed by many luminaries and powerful people. Why didn't it stick?

One possible reason is that it must have been fairly easy to scare landowners into opposition. For example, what would the Roman Catholic church be without the rent from its extensive land holdings? Ditto for other landholding organizations.

Would the same thing happen to co-ownership? It might get people excited initially, but would it take hold and make a practical difference in the world?

The big difference is that co-ownership does not require messing around with taxes nor getting governments into the business of collecting rent. Rather, co-ownership seeks to decentralize the ownership of companies, and this can be done by regular people without government involvement. Undoubtedly, there will be significant opposition to co-ownership, but it won't be easily brushed off as yet another government mandate.

Louis O Kelso

Our suspicion is that the key reason why George's proposal and others like it have not taken root is because they ignored private businesses. Or maybe they didn't ignore businesses but thought of them as a lost cause. Either way, it seems that the biggest miscalculation has been to go straight to government solutions, leaping over businesses.

Henry George was definitely an original thinker, a brilliant observer, and thought well outside the box. He worried and wrote about our lopsided wealth distribution and saw the problem clearly. But when it came to implementation, George, like many others, jumped to the tools of government: regulations, taxes, redistribution. He and many other writers and reformers assumed that businesses could only be changed by coercion, and only the government, the biggest boss of all, could bring enough force to bear to make it happen. Only the government could save the little people from abusive business owners.

The inventor and pioneer of what became known as the Employee Stock Ownership Plans (ESOP), Louis O Kelso, didn't ignore businesses. His big contribution was to figure out how to entice the not-so-enlightened bosses to help workers partake in the wealth created by the companies they worked for.

He was keenly aware that poverty was a human invention, but rather than propping up the poor with handouts, his aim was to eliminate poverty altogether or at least reduce it in a major way. Unfortunately, he, too, ended up getting involved with government.

Kelso was on the right track when he wrote, *"What needs to be adjusted is the opportunity to produce, not the redistribution of income after it's produced."*[59] His idea was to make the workers owners of the businesses they worked for. If businesses are money-making machines, then set it up so that the workers end up as owners of these machines and of the wealth they generate.

However, he made the same mistake that earlier reformers made—he, too, assumed that there had to be a boss and didn't think of eliminating the Fiat hierarchy.

This made the workers financial beneficiaries but not real owners. Ownership is a lot more than financial benefits; it impacts people's lives beyond their work.[60] More important than the monetary gains, owners decide many things that affect employees most often without them knowing it. It is something that most of us never learn about. A home is a passive asset, but home ownership is not the same as being the owner of a productive asset, one that actively generates wealth, like a business.

Part II

An Alternative to the Fiat System

> In the past the man has been first; in the future the system must be first.
>
> — *Frederick W Taylor, The Principles of Scientific Management*

The Radical Foundation

Our deepest problems are the inescapable side-effects of the Fiat system we live in, a system based on domination: our collapsing climate, the wealth gap, discrimination against people of color, the exploitation of women. We need a generative way of relating to one another, a different paradigm. As we see it, companies are the place to start, they are the appropriate incubators for what comes next.

Nature follows a simple path to create big beautiful things out of unpretentious, small ones. From tiny seed to mighty oak tree. We don't think that a long list of principles or color scales or a 17-page constitution are necessary to make a fundamental change. Eventually, these can become dogma and get in the way.

With that in mind, we came up with what we think are the most basic foundations to support our coming together to share work and wealth.

A Three-Legged Stool

Every company is different because the people who embody it are different, so every company must find its own way. Having said that, we do have some opinions as to what fundamentally makes a Radical company different from a Fiat business.

Here's how we see the foundation of a Radical company,

people	**Meaning & Belonging**
community	**Decentralization & Transparency**
practices	**Experimentation**

Other principles and practices can be layered on top of them, but for a Radical company these principles, commitments, and practices are essential, otherwise it is just a Fiat business with ain't-we-nice sprinkled on top.

We have lived in this Fiat world for a long time and the switch to Radical is not going to be instantaneous. As your company changes, you will learn and grow, but staying firm on these tenets will keep you on your path.

Unlike in a Fiat business, a hierarchy is not imposed in a co-managed company. The hierarchies that do emerge are dynamic, fluid, and shaped by what's needed, by the people involved, and a particular time. *"The org chart is insufficient."*[61]

For example, at W L Gore and Associates leaders are selected by their followers. These are real leaders, not money-making-bosses passing as leaders. If people are not happy with the leader or where their effort is heading, they simply leave the team and follow somebody else or start their own projects.[62]

At Valve they do something even more dramatic: desks are on wheels. When people want to leave a team, they roll their desks away,

> Why does your desk have wheels? Think of those wheels as a symbolic reminder that you should always be considering where you could move yourself to be more valuable. But also think of those wheels as literal wheels, because that's what they are, and you'll be able to actually move your desk with them.[63]

At The Morning Star Company people come together around a task and disband when it's done.

In case you are wondering, the result is not chaos at Gore, Valve, or The Morning Star, all of which are financially very successful. Gore has been doing this since 1958, The Morning Star Company since 1970, and Valve since 1997.[64] So, it looks like in addition to being financially successful, these companies are resilient.

Principles: Meaning & Belonging

By Jose Leal

I started several businesses while I was in my late teens and rode the Internet wave all the way to the entrepreneurial dream: the successful exit. After our startup was acquired, my business partner Ron and I joined a top Canadian online media business.

I never thought of myself as a boss but found myself in that situation. I had what many people would consider a dream job—Vice President and General Manager. The business was in the middle of another significant round of growth, hiring executives and hundreds of staff. The corporate budget was nearing dot-com era levels and there was a push for another IPO, the second since I had joined the business. I recall saying, *"I smell greed in the air."*

During the first IPO attempt, I was left to clean up mistakes made as things came to a crashing halt and everyone was thrown off the sinking ship. This time, I watched as those same mistakes were repeated and swore I wasn't going to do it again.

I hated not only the situation I was in but I hated that I had become everything I disliked about corporate types—a political, selfish, hatchet-man. Inwardly, it was killing me and exacting a tremendous toll on my body and personal life. I was a complete mess. Just in time, I was able to negotiate my exit. By the end of that year, the executives and hundreds of staff were gone.

I quickly jumped back in the world of business and co-founded anther startup in the online marketing space. Initially, I was thrilled to be away from corporate life and diving back into a new project. But as I look back on that time, I realize my heart was never in it. Every time things started to look promising, I lost interest. Eventually, both the startup and my marriage were coming to an end, and I was numb to it all.

While spending many months back in Portugal, my birth place, helping to take care of my mother after her stroke, I dove deep into figuring out what had happened. I felt like I was finally starting to come out of the fog I had been in for years. The impact of those ten years had been worse than I had imagined and I couldn't understand how it had happened. How had I become so lost?

I've spent the last several years researching and studying what makes us human and what prompts us to certain actions and choices. Over and over I have found that meaning and belonging are at the center of it all, in a grand loop of interdependence, the human system that connects us and produces our culture. It is what helps people navigate their physical and social world.

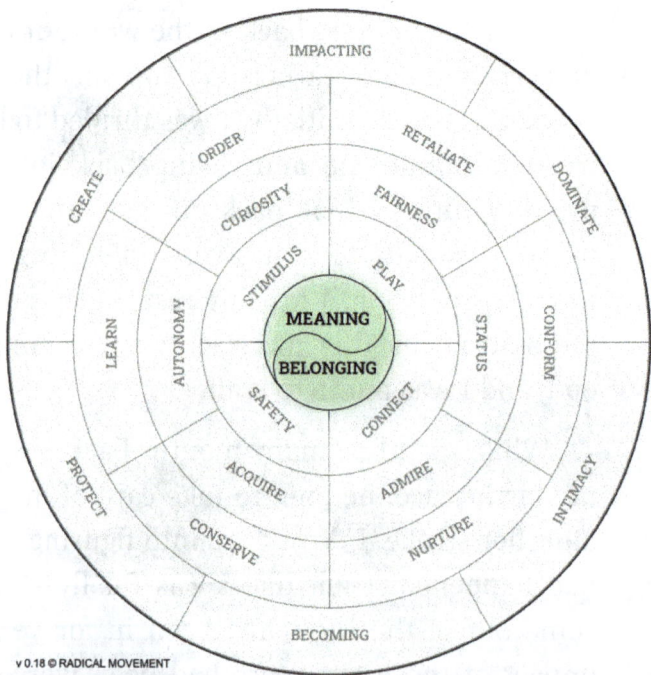

Meaning comes out of stories, and stories come out of your communities, where they make sense. Meaning is what makes sense to each of us, what feels right. As entrepreneur, consultant, and author Chuck Blakeman says, *"people want to make meaning, not just money."*[65] We know when something, an action or act of kindness, is meaningful because it touches us.

I understand that we have to make money to eat, to pay the rent, to pay for school, to get to work. But what drives us is making sense of the world around us and discovering with others the many ways in which we can live our lives and apply our potential without hurting anyone. In a study published in Frontiers in Psychology, Hu and Hirsh found that *"... participants reported minimum acceptable salaries that were 32% lower for personally meaningful jobs compared to jobs that were perceived as personally meaningless."*[66]

Artists do their work because, to them, it is meaningful, even cathartic. They may or may not make a living at it, but they keep at it. All meaningful work is self-expression, it is art.

People know that they belong when they are aligned with the group. People know that they belong when they feel safe and can count on other people's support because they understand each other's struggles. And it works in virtual communities, too, as in this tweet,

> **Alex "Warmly From 10 Feet Away" Anderson**
> @AlexAndersonMD
>
> Thanks for being so incredibly nice and showing me grace when I share my weakness, failures, insecurities, etc here. Seriously thank you.
>
> 8:40 PM · May 9, 2020 · Twitter for iPhone

67

Author and consultant Nilofer Merchant[68] captured how meaning and belonging are two sides of the proverbial coin.

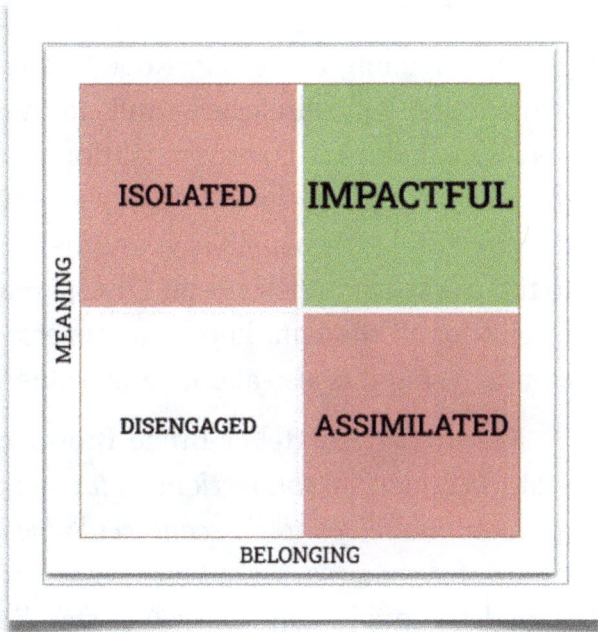

Transparency & Decentralization

By Matt Perez

I spent most of my working life hiding things: information, actions, decisions, mistakes. I could make decisions that my subordinates couldn't. I am pretty sure that I made decisions that they could have made if only they had access to the right information. I certainly didn't want to repeat that at Nearsoft.

After reading *Maverick*, Roberto and I agreed to practice full disclosure and to decentralize decision-making. Decentralization was about opening things up so that everybody can make decisions, take responsibility, and be accountable to themselves and their peers. Transparency meant disclosing all the data known or generated by the company, but it is also about being vulnerable.

Researcher-storyteller Brené Brown points out that, "*in order for connections to happen, we have to allow ourselves to be seen—really seen.*"[69] This means, for example, asking for help when you need it, and accepting help even when you didn't know you needed it.

It is impossible to decentralize decision-making without making the necessary information transparent. And transparency without decentralization is simply frustrating, like seeing the candy behind that glass that you cannot reach.

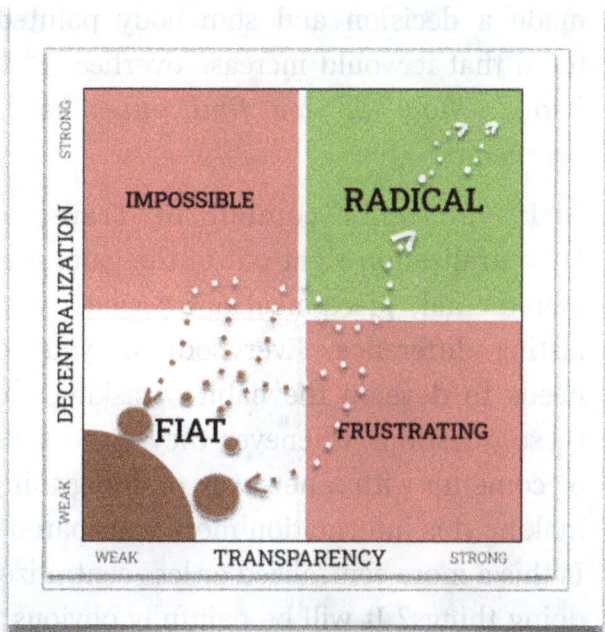

A four-quadrant diagram with axes DECENTRALIZATION (vertical, WEAK to STRONG) and TRANSPARENCY (horizontal, WEAK to STRONG). Quadrants labeled: IMPOSSIBLE (top-left), RADICAL (top-right), FIAT (bottom-left), FRUSTRATING (bottom-right).

70

From my own experience at Nearsoft, you can never be 100% transparent or decentralized. Not because you don't want to, but because you can't see what you can't see. Even though we were very committed to both at Nearsoft, we found things that are not as transparent or decentralized as we would like them to be.

For example, Roberto and I decided on budgets by ourselves until somebody said something like, *"These numbers are not going to work! Why didn't you ask me?"* So we decentralized the budgeting process. In another instance, a group made a decision and somebody pointed out to them that it would increase overhead. *"We didn't know... how do we find out what impacts overhead?"*

If you don't commit to Transparency & Decentralization right out of the gate, none of the incremental, piece-meal approaches will make a lasting difference. Everybody in your company needs to develop the habit of asking themselves these questions whenever they write a document or come up with a new way of doing things. Am I making this information more transparent or less? Is this a more centralized or less centralized way of doing things? It will be painfully obvious to you if decisions that are important to you become more centralized or if somebody is purposely hiding information that's important for you and others to know. You'll feel it in your body when a particular task stops making sense to you but you have to keep doing it, or when you are forced to conform to the group norms, but have no voice in the matter.

Don't worry if you are the only one who's noticed any of these threats. That's what makes you valuable to your group. Help them notice. Diversity is the collection of fears that renders them all powerless.

Alignment & Experimentation

By Adrian Perez

I have always been interested in what I would call the Third Way. It has seemed to me that often when both sides are getting it wrong. You have two sides that are pushing and pulling over some territory and they get stuck. This usually serves both sides because it validates their survival. Whether it is traditional school or Montessori, Communism versus Capitalism, or any other such conflict, I look for the third way.

In the case of schools, I found Sudbury Schools and Summersill. And for the case of how humans should organize their businesses, I have helped conceive the ideas in this book that we call Radical. The idea is to end the game that no longer serves us so we can create a whole new game. I enjoy shaking off the older system and removing the old impediments to human happiness, resilience, and personal power.

ESOPs	An ESOP provides the legal basis for approximating universal equity ownership. But the ESOP must be set to really operate with the full participation of the co-owners and that is almost never the case. New Belgium Brewery came closest and then it got acquired by Kirin.
open book management	Open Book Management provides financial transparency and so it seems to fit the co-ownership model. It illustrates that transparency is not just making the numbers available and posting them on the walls. People need to know how to read these numbers and how to figure out what it means to them as well as to the company. But it doesn't require equity ownership or any other real ownership. People learn to read the books, but they don't get to participate in the decisions that shape them.
co-operatives, LCAs	Every member owns an equal piece of the co-op, but they don't necessarily participate in strategic decisions. One member, one vote is irrelevant without co-management. What matters is that members get to participate in shaping the questions, not just voting for A or B. In the Radical co-ownership model not all co-owners own the same percentage; their fellow co-owners decide the value of their contributions.

Having worked in software businesses in Silicon Valley, some growing and some collapsing, I have experienced the very informal and yet still very hierarchical, unimaginative, and stifling environments of corporate America. We can do better.

It will take operating at our best to pull ourselves out of the nosedive that global civilization finds itself in. And it starts with explicit alignment.

Explicit Alignment is what gets everybody to paddle in the same direction. You must make a habit of listening to the passionate voices in the group and embrace the vision that emerges.

For a Fiat business, Impact and Purpose pretty much collapses to *"generate wealth for the Fiat owner"* and its Mission is whatever the boss wants, and where the boss wants it. For a Radical company, an explicit alignment does a better job of helping a group of people move in the same direction. With it in hand, adults can figure out how best to contribute. No boss needed, thank you.

Experimentation is the practice that gives shape to all other practices. Every proposal and every crazy idea must end up with something like, *"should we try it?"* Once asking this question becomes a habit, not doing it will feel odd, like something is missing. Experiment with any practice that you think will work, but experiment.

You'll get to experiment with all the things that are usually required at work, including, among many others, schedules, and location. For example, COVID-19 has forced the whole world to explore whether or not we need an office. Some people say that we'll never go back to offices, but others miss the social aspects of it.

But even if we get physically together to work, does it have to be every day, every other day, or as needed? Does it have to be *at the office*" or could it be elsewhere, anywhere?

Experiment and find out what practices best support what works for you. Find your Third Way.

Explicit Alignment

The Scout Salute

When it is just you and a couple of friends on a walk, the direction is set quasi-randomly by one of you and the others follow as you all talk. No big deal. But creating a service or making a product is more complex than a walk in the park. We will need a robust, scalable way of deciding what to build and how to do it.

In order to create a Radical company, we will first need to be explicit about the company's *what for*, its *why*, and it's *what, how,* and *when*. You might call them something different or you might lump some of these together. However you express them, they have to be explicit and completely open and accessible to everyone.

The three-finger Scout Salute[71] is a good mnemonic for remembering the elements of an Explicit Alignment,

Explic

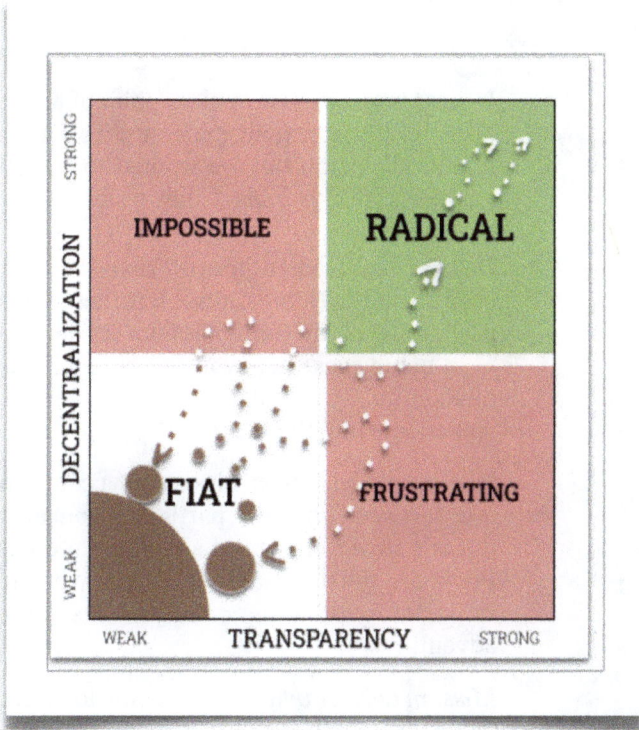

it

Alignment

For a company to have a well understood, explicit alignment as to what you are intent on doing as a community of co-owners. You need to explain to new, and old, co-owners *what you are doing this for* and *why*.

It is very easy to fall back to Fiat when the task ahead of you seems impossible or gets frustrating.

- *Impact* is our beacon, a clear point of light just over the horizon that guides us. This is what many call Vision but we wanted to put more emphasis on the impact that vision will have on the world.

  Dave Logan, lead author of Tribal Leadership, used to call it Noble Cause, but these days he prefers to call it Noble Passion. As he puts it, "... a noble cause gets you out of bed. A noble passion gets you out of bed early and keeps you up late into the night."

- *Purpose* is the reason why we, as a community are focused on this particular journey. It doesn't have to be world shaking. An effective Purpose must clearly express why it is important for others to join us in this adventure.

- *Mission* defines *what* we are going to do to move towards the Impact, *how* we are going to do it, and by *when*. In the case of Nearsoft, everybody takes part in this: about 80 Nearsoftians in the first one, and around 300 participated in defining the second.

This is but one way to express Alignment. The important thing is to make it explicit and easy to understand to everybody in the team. I should be able to ask anybody in the team, *"What is our company's Foundation?"* and get very similar answers, not totally different answers.

To do their job, to be effective, and present to everybody, our alignment choices have to be baked into everything we actually do. Otherwise they are reduced to nice words on the wall collecting dust.

Values?

The other thing that we'd have to think about is Values.

This is not about the *"Our Values"* poster in the lobby. These are usually meaningless stuff. Something the boss came up with. They normally get weaponized, *"I hear that you are not much of a team player, didn't you know that being a team player is one of our values?"*

Values were very much in vogue as a tool of alignment and so in 2010, inspired by Tony Hsieh, we came up with our Values as a business. Back then, there were about 40 of us. We broke up into groups of five to seven people and we played a couple of Innovation Games, starting with Trim the Product Tree.[72] As its name implies, this tool is meant to create a list of important product features, but it worked quite well for our purpose of coming up with a list of what was important to us as a group.

Our understanding back then is that these (uppercase) Values applied to the whole company, in any situation, at any time. These days, I believe that (lowercase) values are more relevant when associated with a process that makes them alive and relevant.

Be careful to stay away from vague, feel-good words. For example, in the case of recruiting at Nearsoft we evaluate the candidate on each value on a one-to-four scale to discover each interviewer's perception of the candidate and have pointed conversations about big gaps, if any.

Process and values are the yin and yang of effective execution. If you can't identify what makes a process valuable, then you are probably following a bureaucratic procedure.

Nearsoft Values ended up describing the qualities we wanted future Nearsoftians to have.[73] As luck would have it, *Teamwork, Leadership, Commitment, Smart, Gets things done,* and *Long-term relationships.* These were as appealing and meaningful to our clients as they were to us because they describe the qualities we both look for in people.

Over time, other things come up regularly during the recruiting process,[74] like curiosity and resourcefulness. A comment like, "... *I was interested, but they didn't teach me*," usually is a red flag (*i.e.*, not a self-learner). Did she talk about things that she had learned on her own or by reaching out to more experienced people? Or were all her answers some version of, "*they didn't send me to that course?*" By now, *curiosity* and *autodidact* have become part of our de facto values of the hiring process.

We use our values-as-checklist at the end of the interview process, during what we call our Thumbs meeting. At this meeting, all the people who talked to the candidate get together and each interviewer grades the candidate on a 1-4 scale along two axes: skills and cultural alignment.

Most of the time, all the interviewers line up, but every so often, we have trouble coming to an agreement. And that's where having these Values is useful. Are we talking about *leadership* or *commitment* issues? Was it apparent that she didn't care about *long-term relationships*?

Every so often, somebody says, *"but, she doesn't have a degree!"* even though it's not in our list of Values. But that is easily dealt with, the same way I was disabused of that 'requirement' a while back,

- Did she know her tech stuff?

- Did she come up short against any of our values?

- Didn't she demonstrate curiosity?

- Doesn't the fact that she learned a bunch of skills pretty much by herself show that she is smart and resourceful?

- Then, what's with the *"degree?"*

I am not so sure that there is a short list of core values that apply to the whole company; in fact, I doubt it. On the other hand, I am very sure that each key process needs a checklist associated with it that defines what makes it valuable. The process of coming up with these values, itself, provides clarity and creates a common commitment to the goals of a given process.

In our new Radical company it would make sense to experiment to find values for key processes.

Radical Distribution

For over 100 years many have been aware of the problems with our model of Fiat ownership. As we've mentioned, the followers of Marx tried one way of solving it, but that made matters worse. Others, like Olivetti in Italy and others in Europe, tried the paternalistic approach, but that didn't last. Still others have championed the cooperative model of equal ownership, but that has not taken the world by fire, either.

On the other side of the coin, the joint-stock business, a capitalist invention, has been very, very financially successful. That's the system where businesses sell shares of themselves to investors. Having individuals pool their money to fund big projects is one of the foundations of capitalism. The financial markets are all about this and so is Venture Capital.

For example, a baker wants to make a giant cake (the joint-stock company). I and others (investors) buy the ingredients in exchange for a share of the cake's sale price. *"I bought him sugar for $1 and I got $1.50 in return when the cake was sold."* Or maybe I can't wait until the cake is sold, so I sell my share of the cake to you, another investor, for $1.25; later, you get $1.50 when the cake is sold. It's a sweet deal all around, and you don't have to be very particularly wealthy to be part of this, but you have to have money that you don't mind losing if the cake doesn't sell or is sold for less than expected.

But what about the baker's helpers? They don't have any money to spare and they get their wages, but none of the extra wealth that they helped create. If he is feeling generous, maybe the baker can give them some of his shares. Or the investors are willing to chip in to some shares for the workers. Or maybe the government can dictate that a percentage of the sale be divided equally among the workers. Note that in all these cases,

- Some people, one or a few, decide for others. They choose what and how much to give (i.e., the government counts as one person).

- The worth of each share is static, fixed at the beginning of this process and way before the cake is baked.

- The number of shares the workers get, if they get any, is arbitrary.

- The government mandate may be egalitarian but not likely equitable.

The option of letting the workers decide is anathema to the Fiat mindset. It is simply unthinkable and too scary to be considered for more than a fleeting moment. "*It would be too chaotic.*" But so-called labor is as important as capital in making new things happen.

The Distribution mechanism we describe below makes ownership decentralized and dynamic. It supports distribution of wealth based on *contribution*. And it is scalable.

Rosedale Distribution

Rosedale Distribution is our name for a practice that I first heard from entrepreneur Philip Rosedale, founder of Linden Labs, High Fidelity, and several other companies in between. He came up with this scheme in 2005 when Linden had about 50 employees. It goes like this,

- As the company grows, cash and shares are put out for distribution every month.

- Every member gets, say, $1,000, an equal portion of the wealth the company generated.

- People don't get to keep these goodies for themselves, but they get to distribute them to other members.

- They give it to anybody they feel has contributed the most during the month, whether or not they are an employee.

- Each person decides how much to give to whom based on whatever criteria feels right at that time. Each person knows best who has contributed.

Manas, a company in Argentina does something very similar. They knew nothing of Rosedale's system and independently came up with a similar system. This goes to show that others are moving in the same direction, albeit somewhat haphazardly.

Radical Distribution

The Radical Distribution is based on the Rosedale Distribution. In both cases, everyone has a direct hand in doing something that is usually reserved for owners—wealth and ownership distribution—and they get in the habit of doing so.

The Radical Distribution process is scalable. Thanks to telephone apps, thousands of people can distribute wealth and ownership the same way that a handful can.

Instead of cash or stocks, Radical Distribution uses a dimensionless unit we call a RAD. Whereas money has a fixed value, RADs factor value through them. Whereas stocks represent a fixed percentage of the company forever, RADs represent a dynamic percentage of ownership at each cycle (*e.g.*, monthly). And they represent *any* kind of contribution, not just financial.

RADs account for the uncountable.

The Radical Distribution has an *egalitarian* component and an *equitable* component. The egalitarian piece is that everyone gets an equal number of RADs which represent an equal portion of what they have created together. Co-owners then get to distribute these RADs according to their individual judgement. Each decides what is an equitable number of RADs to give to other co-owners as recognition for their contributions. The value of the whole emerges from the judgement of the many.

A few important observations,

- RADs are not a currency.

- RADs are issued before there is revenue because contributions happen regardless of revenue.

- The giving criteria is completely up to each person, although we can agree to some explicit guiding criteria to start with. In any case, at Distribution Retrospectives new criteria are fleshed out and harvested as an optional guideline.

- RADs represent dynamic ownership. One month you may give me all your RADs, but the next month you may not give me any.

- The absolute number of RADs allocated to me either stays the same or goes up at every distribution. If I had 100 RADs last cycle and I get 50 this cycle, my total number of RADs goes to 150. If I don't get any this cycle, my total number of RADs stays at 100.

  On the other hand, my percentage of the total could go up, stay the same, or go down at every Distribution. If my 100 RADs represented 10% of the total last cycle and I get 150 RADs this cycle, then my percent ownership went up to 12.5%; if I get 100 new RADs, my percentage stays at 10%; if don't get any new RADs, my percentage goes down to 5%.

- To calculate your percentage ownership, divide the number of RADs you have been allocated by the total number of allocated RADs.

- When money, or time, or whatever else is disbursed later, it is done as a function of the number of RADs each person owns. If you have accumulated 200 RADs and I have 100, then you'll get twice as much as me of whatever is being factored through the RADs.

There probably are many ways of doing this,

- *Each cycle* each member gets to distribute a number of RADs as they see fit. For example, if you get 100 RADs this month, you may give fifty to Adrian, 30 to Jose, and 20 to me.

As always, you'll have to experiment to see what works for you.

Scalability

Because Distributions are decentralized, scalability is not an issue. As Phil Rosedale points out, "... *if you let everybody in the company impose their own bias on the situation but you give them all an equal amount of money, all the biases cancel each other out and the only coherent signal that remains is: I want the company to be around.*"[75]

One person's point of view: 17 of 56 people.

2: 11 of 56   3: 40 of 56   4: 55 of 56   5: 56 of 56

People are the best judges of who should be recognized and what should be recognized as a contribution.

As people share and give each other RADs, they learn the value of what they've built together at a visceral level. They will learn from their peers to value of what they do, their accomplishments.

People will be encouraged to learn to communicate better (*"It ain't bragging if you've done it"*[76]). They will learn to talk about their failures, what they've learned from them, and how it can be valuable to others.

Phil Rosedale puts his finger on the key point, *"If you know your peers are going to judge you each quarter freely and give money to you, you'll probably work at being more transparent."*[77]

Equality vs Equity

After we had written about Radical Distributions, we ran into a study by DeVoe and Iyengar where they conclude that, *"people view it as less fair to distribute resources equally when the allocated resource invokes the market by being a medium of exchange than when the allocated resource is a good that holds value in use."*[78] In other words, giving everybody $12 regardless of contribution is more likely to be seen as unfair than giving everybody a dozen carrots. The carrots can only be eaten, maybe traded, whereas the $12 can be saved, used to pay credit card debt, or used to buy something online.

Radical Distributions

Radical Distributions let each co-owner allocate RADs as they see fit. Equality is not the goal. The resulting allocations will most likely not be equal, but they'll be equitable ,

- What each co-owner recognizes as a contribution
- How valuable that contribution is to co-owners.

Every co-owner has a different view of what equitable is and will be able to express it in tangible ways through RAD allocations.

New Features

In the Rosedale Distribution, 1) the criteria for "what's equitable" remains inside people's heads, and 2) it's all about individuals, not teams.

To address these issues, we added *Banners* to Radical Distributions to give everybody an opportunity to recognize teams and other nonpersons like special accomplishments, projects, causes, etc.

Retrospectives

At a Radical Retrospective members could discuss the criteria they used to allocate RADs. Participation in these Retrospectives is voluntary and members can share their criteria.

This may range from *"I gave mine to people who worked with me on..."* to *"I was feeling depressed and the person I gave most of my RADs to was there for me."* These criteria are documented and published for others to learn from and consider them at future distributions, if they wish. Over time, this serves as a training mechanism for members, particularly the new ones who are not yet used to doing owner things. It does not prevent people from making their own decisions, but it serves as a guide.

Feedback

There has been a lot of research on the dynamics of power and status in relationships.

Power is the ability to realize one's interest. Status enhances another person's stature. Power exacts compliance and status invites cooperation. Both are an *"equally stable and predictable"* social structure, according to social psychologist Michael R A Chance.[79]

Radical Distributions work because people like to give (power) and receive (status). In as much as the giving and receiving of RADs is a form of recognition. Distributions *"will reflect on one's own power and status... and on the power and status of the other."*[80]

By giving, my own power goes up (*i.e.*, without diminishing anybody else's power). Everybody in the company gets to experience the joy of giving and the jolt of power that goes with it. In the status dimension, it is a bit more complicated. If you get more than you expected, everything's peachy and you're overjoyed, *"There appears to be nothing like the joy of unexpected rewards."*[81] But if you get less than expected, *"anger and depression can both result from an episode of status loss."*[82] Instead we can turn these situations into learning opportunities. In particular, people who didn't get less than they expected would want to do this. It might be difficult to hear the feedback, but it's the way to grow. It can help resolve latent tensions, correct wrong impressions, and get better results in the future.

Banners

At Nearsoft, anybody could make up whatever title they wanted for themselves. However, that's not the same as being recognized by others. I confused the two for a long time. Recognition is really important to both the giver and the receiver. Whether as individuals or as a team, having our accomplishments recognized by others is very important and precious to people.

Banners can stand for teams, special accomplishments, communities, new products, etc.

teams	Teams can be represented by a Banner. "Recognize our IT support team for how they handled the storm."
special accomplishments	Margot deserves to be recognized for stewarding the creation of our training platform.
community	For example, a 'no noise' Banner could fund a sound barrier around a noisy factory.

experimental projects	At one point Google got a lot of coverage for their policy of allowing everybody the use 20% of their time to work o side projects. Things like Google News came of it. That a generous policy given the Fiat owner, by the same owners later took it away, quietly. For a Radical company the equivalent thing would be to put up a Banner that co-owners could allocate RADs to it as they see fit.
investments	In Fiat businesses the owners can decide whether or not to, say, purchase a new office building. Maybe it is done as a wise investment, or maybe it has more to do with ego, like a pharaoh's pyramid. In a Radical company, anybody can put up a New building Banner and allow co-owners to contribute to the funding of it or not.

Radical Distributions

> *"Will everybody know who I gave RADs to and how many? Will they know how many I got and from whom?"*

The fear behind these questions is not irrational: disclosing your salary can get you in big trouble at a Fiat business. It's a taboo subject and you may have even convinced yourself that the secrecy is for your own good. No wonder some people are fearful about it.

These kinds of questions are very similar to the ones that sometimes came up when we told people that at Nearsoft our salaries were open to anybody. As of the time I left, there are over 900 Nearsoftians and I can count on one hand the number of people who have voiced concerns over this. We've never had to hide anybody's salary.

Complete Transparency

We don't think that Radical Distributions will work without complete transparency. In theory, the allocator and recipient could block their identity or the number of RADs allocated, but that is fear speaking. We don't think that anything less than full disclosure will work.

Of course, you'll have to figure out what works for you, but hiding any of this information is likely to turn out to be a failure (*i.e.*, who knows the real numbers?)

Accounting for the Uncountable

RADs represent many things other than simple financial value. They are not beans, but they can be counted.

The RADs you have represent how other people feel about you and how they value your contributions. If you are making us miserable, you'll probably get fewer RADs; if you are helping us, you'll likely get more. If you do something that goes against, for example, our Impact. *"but, hey, it will makes money,"* you'll probably get less RADs; on the other hand, if you introduce a way to make more money *and* strengthen our alignment, you'll get more RADs.

In short, RADs account for the uncountable, they measure the immeasurable.

Co-Ownership, Co-Management

Co-Ownership

Co-ownership, too, is blocked by the Fiat hierarchy. Cooperatives are a good example of that. For example, Mondragon, the biggest co-op on planet Earth, is run by a traditional Fiat hierarchy. Even though workers are the financial owners, they have little participation in strategic decisions. At Mondragon and other cooperatives, the workers may be well taken care of, but they are not full owners. This type of ownership is what Dr Corey Rosen calls *symbolic ownership* in *his book*

Ownership, people enjoy financial benefits but nothing else. Co-ownership requires participation in strategic and structural decisions that affect the overall company. It's not only about knowing how to read the books, but getting involved in decisions that have an impact on said books.

To work, ownership must be decentralized and broadly distributed to everybody who contributes to the company.

In a conversation with author and self-management coach Chuck Blakeman, I once bemoaned the fact that co-management by itself was way too dependent on *"enlightened monarchs,"* owners committed to co-management. But co-management ends when the benign boss walks off the stage.

Chuck certainly is one of the enlightened ones. He has led co-management *"in twelve businesses, in eight industries, on four continents."*[83] These days, among other things, he trains and coaches people on their co-management journey.

Back when we had that conversation I couldn't think of any way of doing co-management without a benevolent boss. Without co-ownership, co-management happens *"at the pleasure of"* the Fiat owner and a new, not-so-enlightened owner can easily revert to traditional Fiat management. No matter how you slice it, the owner is the boss,

> **Jack Riminton**
> @jackrim1
>
> Replying to @3dfordesigners
>
> To 'flat management' etc I always follow the money, who's got the biggest equity stake? There's your boss
>
> 2:20 PM · Feb 5, 2020 · Twitter for iPhone

84

Co-ownership removes co-management's dependence on an owner. It replaces Fiat ownership and decentralizes the kind of power and distributes its power. Everyone who contributes to the company is a co-owner of it. They are not symbolic owners and their voices actively count when it comes to reserved-for-owners decisions.

At home, people behave a certain way because it *is* their home and they *own it* beyond the legal sense. They belong there. They feel entitled to ask questions and know what's going on. They feel responsible for fixing things. Each member of the household is accountable to the others.

At work, Fiat owners behave similarly, with a sense of entitlement and responsibility. Everybody else is working for a wage. Full-time, part-time, or on-demand. Salaried, per hour, per widget, or on commission. Even well-paid superstars and big time execs. All of them work *"at the pleasure of"* the Fiat owner. Fiat ownership is the reason why our businesses are so inefficient and make us all miserable. Co-ownership aims to break this cycle by decentralizing ownership and making people co-owners of the companies they embody. It leverages ownership, a foundation of capitalism, and makes it broadly available. It makes people active participants in financial ***and*** decision making, not just the recipients of financial benefits.

ESOPs and co-operatives are not co-ownership because they focus on the money end of things but say nothing about who runs things or how. *"More money for us!"* is not sufficient. Money may be what keeps me awake at night if I don't have enough of it, but it's not what makes me spring out of bed in the morning. And it's definitely not what fills me with pride and satisfaction at the end of the day.

Co-ownership is about having everybody in a company walk around with a sense of entitlement, responsibility, and accountability about their workplace. Because they own it.

What Does an Owner Own?

These are some of the decisions that a Fiat owner may make (or has veto power over),

fate of the company	• Are we going to sell the company? • Are we going to merge with another business?
strategy	• What business should we be in? • Do we stay in that niche? • Do we expand to an adjacent area? • How do we position our products?
how to deal with bad times	• What to do during times of flat or negative growth? • Do we borrow? How much? • Do we take capital investments? • How much and for what percentage of the company? • Do we lay off people? How many? Who?

In addition, the owner also has the final word on these decisions,

investment	• Are we going to sell the company • Are we going to grow our current business? • Are we going to invest in a new or adjacent business? • Do we borrow money? How much and from whom? • How much will we spend on training?
capital allocation	• What do we do with year's profit? • Do I, as owner, take it all or most of it? • Do we grow our operations next year? • Do we reserve some for Earned Dividends? • Do we fund a new office?
share distribution	• Do I give/sell shares of the company? • How many? For how much? Who? When? • What is the criteria?
wealth extraction	• How much is reserved for the owners? • Should we implement Profit Sharing? • How do we handle salaries, raises?

We have been conditioned to believe that *regular people* cannot deal with these issues, only the gifted amongst us can. These gifted people deserve the rewards of their special talent. So it must have taken me a long time to become gifted because it took me six businesses before the seventh was financially successful. Or maybe I was gifted all along, but it took me a while to *"embrace my gift."* The reality is that *"talent is overrated. Skills are acquirable."*[85]

There was no gift involved. I've been very lucky and privileged, but I am not that special. And I am not saying that out of false modesty. I think the world of me, but I still learn new lessons every day from those around me. And it wasn't *magic* that made Nearsoft successful, it took a lot of work from a lot of people.

So maybe the people whose labor makes a company grow and thrive, maybe they could learn what about ownership in a company to have a voice in it and make even significant contributions. And maybe the whole thing about the gift is a convenient story that we accept as fact, *even though it isn't*.

Co-ownership gives every member the chance to learn to become an owner *in every sense of the word*. Not everybody will start at the same level, not everybody will be equally interested, and not everybody will learn at the same rate. But co-ownership provides the training ground for members to develop as owners.

Transparency & Decentralization

Jack Stack, an enthusiastic champion of Open-Book Management, makes the point that he had to learn these things on his own because the company he worked for didn't think he was trustworthy enough. He was a general manager, *"You begin to realize that this is not rocket science, that I could understand these metrics... I'd get angry at the company I worked for because in the 14 years I worked there, the company didn't think I could understand those metrics..."*[86]

By whatever name it goes, lack of transparency is the culprit. As Mr Stack discovered, transparency is required in order to make decisions. You have to teach *"people the metrics of a great company."*[87]

In the late 1970s Ricardo Semler had a similar realization at SEMCO: regular people, with a basic education could learn to understand the company's finances. *"All financial information at Semco is openly discussed... workers have unlimited access to our books... with the labor unions that represent our workers, we developed a course to teach everyone, even messengers and cleaning people, to read balance sheets and cash flow statements."*[88]

Other things, like hiring and firing, can be handled by regular people on their own, without a boss-as-babysitter. Bosses impose themselves at work and it and makes it less efficient and productive.

The Case for Co-ownership

From the onset, Nearsoft has been a grand experiment where we've tried out lots of ways to co-managed as peers. We also took a couple of steps into what I recognize now as co-ownership. However, co-ownership had no name then and we didn't get far enough on that path.

Ownership is something that most of us never learn about. Particularly, ownership of a productive asset, like a business (*i.e.*, home ownership is not the same as being the owner of an asset that actively generates wealth).

Without co-ownership, co-management is tenuous and always "*at the pleasure of*" the Fiat owners. No matter how well-intended these folks are, it all comes to an end when they are no longer the owners. Co-ownership is the way out of that trap. It does not depend on taxes or new laws or other government actions. It is not a call for the end of Capitalism. What's radical about co-ownership is that it does not require a serious reshaping of ownership, one of the foundations of Capitalism. It only requires that ownership is more broadly distributed.

The Not-So-Hidden Hand

As Adam Smith laid out in *The Wealth of Nations*, the market started as a *decentralized pricing machine*, although over time it has turned into a gambling table. Capital tends to concentrate into fewer and fewer hands and financial markets are not the level-playing field we believe they are.[89]

Even if the outcome of every transaction is chosen by a fair coin flip, many such sales and purchases will inevitably result in all the wealth falling into the hands of a single person—leading to a situation of extreme inequality.[90]

Bernard Lietaer, an economist, author, and professor, studied monetary systems. With co-author Jacqui Dunne he makes a convincing case that this imbalance has a lot to do with interest bearing currency.

Because of the upward concentration of wealth caused by interest, there was a transfer of wealth from the bottom 80 percent of the population to the top 20 percent, especially the top 10 percent, due exclusively to the interest feature of the monetary system used.

> This transfer of wealth occurred independently of the cleverness or industriousness of the participants, attributes often assumed to account for differences in income.
>
> This, in turn, makes a mockery of the very concept of free markets, as no one is really free in such a system.[91]

You don't have to go far for the evidence: as of this writing the richest 62 people *own* half of the world's wealth.[92] Decisions are made for the sake of more possessions and riches and little else. We can try and change the monetary system or we can regulate the heck out of it. We think the thing to do is to decentralize our ownership model. This option is the most practical and most effective.

As company ownership spreads and the decision-making authority and habits that comes with it broadens, we all will be better for it. For example, Climate Change would have been dealt with a long time ago.

Full Ownership

As we've said, being an owner is far more than just being a financial beneficiary. Full owners take an active part in running the company, including financial and strategy decisions.

There have been mild attempts to broaden ownership, but they all end up not going far enough.

The Symbolic Ownership Tragedy

In 2014 Fagor,[93] the business that launched what's today known as Mondragon, was on a financial losing streak. Its market was changing dramatically and other appliance manufacturers had closed down or were about to. Evidently, management felt that with more capital they could outlast what they perceived as a temporary crisis.

In order to save the business, they proposed to use their internal capital to subsidize their operation. As a progressive coop they put it to a vote, and it was approved by their worker-*owners*. What these nominal owners didn't seem to understand is that this *"internal capital"* included their social funds for retirement, savings, education, etc. Or maybe they did, but, hey, if management wanted to do it, then it must be OK.

Two years later, in 2016, Fagor threw in the towel and shut down. Most everybody got jobs with other Mondragon coops, but their Fagor social funds were wiped out.

The symbolic owners took to the streets to demonstrate against a decision that they themselves had agreed to.

"IN DEFENSE OF OUR JOBS"

It seems that these *workers* did not feel like full owners. They went along with their management on the belief, my guess, that they would be OK. When it became obvious that that was not the case, they felt betrayed and took to the streets.

Financial participation is *symbolic* ownership, not co-ownership.

Then, What Is Co-Ownership?

Co-owners have equity in their company and participate in financial and strategy decisions. Anything short of this is not co-ownership.

Many of the existing approaches may be a step in the right direction. They may be generous and possibly better than the norm. But without ownership and full participation in decision making it is not co-ownership. These programs, by themselves, don't represent co-ownership.

As a counterexample, for as long as it remained independent the New Belgium Brewery combined an ESOP and Openbook Management practices to create a semblance of co-ownership. And, then the company got sold to Kirin. The tenured people got compensated, including those who were no longer employees.

As of this writing, we can only think of W L Gore as a co-owned and co-managed company. Namasté Solar may be as well.

BuurtzorgT[94] is well on its way.[95] Founded by Jos de Blok and Nico Moleman in 2013, BuurtzorgT grew very quickly and they needed capital to sustain its growth. Instead of the usual suspects, they found an investor that was open to Steward Ownership, *"a viable alternative to shareholder-primacy ownership"*[96]

People-Centered Financial Strategy

In money-first terms, financial ownership works, *"A 2000 Rutgers study found that ESOP companies grow 2.3% to 2.4% faster after setting up their ESOP than would have been expected without it."*[97] And so is co-management, *"... world-class freedom-centered cultures based on the principles of organizational democracy... deliver 7x revenue growth (on average) compared to S&P 500 companies."*[98]

When combining co-management with co-ownership, a company's financial performance could be much higher. For example, the NCEO reports that even companies with a limited form of participation *"grow 8% to 11% per year faster with their ownership plans than they would have without them."*[99]

In other words, putting people at the center of it all happens to be the smarter financial strategy, too.

Co-Management

Co-management means that you and your co-workers are responsible for creating a company that works for everybody. There is no pre-packaged solution, only a lot of work and lots of experimentation to figure out what works for each unique group of people.

In a Fiat business, you just ask the boss. In a co-managed company, you don't have a boss and you and your co-workers have to come up with the answers. Be careful not to replace a Fiat hierarchy of individuals with a bureaucracy. There's no difference between *"because I say so"* and *"because given the rules stated on page 32 of the*

47-page document that you signed..." They are both Fiat, centralized mechanisms used to exert control.

There is no prescribed series of steps to get started. Help create a community of people and learn from them. What's most important is that whatever you start with does not become dogma. You will make a pile of mistakes and that's the way it is. You will learn from each mistake more than from any 'Bible.'

Ben and Jerry

Although we present co-ownership and co-management as two separate concepts, in reality they are inseparable, two sides of the same coin. Bonnie and Clyde. Sherlock Holmes and Dr Watson. Ben and Jerry. One without the other is not enough to impact the current narrative of our lives. One without the other does not have the sustained transformative effect we need in order to move forward.

In a Fiat company, co-management exists *"at the pleasure of"* the company's benevolent boss. Any form of financial benefit in a Fiat managed company is tenuous at best and, again, *"at the pleasure of"* the boss.

In the past, there have been a number of European companies that modeled and promoted wealth sharing (*e.g.*, Olivetti in Italy, John Lewis and Scott Barder in the UK, Endenburg Electric in the Netherlands). They embraced a form of symbolic ownership but maintained a Fiat hierarchy in charge.

Take John Lewis Partnership in England. John Spedan Lewis, the son of the store's founder, turned all his shares of the company to a Trust owned by the company's employees, which he called partners. That made them the owners of the company and were entitled to receive the dividends that would have gone to Lewis and his family. However, he left the hierarchy in place. Lewis created a *"highly elaborate governance structure comprising a series of forums, councils and internal publications"*[100] as a check on management. Today the bosses are in control of the company.

Earnest Bader, founder of Scott Bader, sold all his and his family's shares to a company Trust and ceded all would-be dividends to the employees. But like John Lewis, he left a Fiat hierarchy in place. Here, too, the bosses have warped the company in their favor.

Less known is that Olivetti, the Italian typewriter company, *"was once a model for workers' rights."*[101] The system Adrianno Olivetti put in place survived him for 28 years but in the end it failed. Had co-ownership been in place, it might have prevented what eventually happened: a downstream CEO dismantled what Adriano called the *co-determination system.*

Gerard Endenburg, founder of Endenburg Electric, became the poster child of Sociocracy and became an active promoter. He was inspired by the work of Kees Boeke and Beatrice Cadbury Boeke to put Sociocratic Democracy[102] to work at Endenburg Electric. Endenburg put his shares in a foundation for the benefit of employees. However, he also left in place a hierarchy. He hoped that "... *the interlocking circles provide a check against its excesses."*[103] It didn't.

Further back, Wm. Filene Son's Co, a US retail empire, created the Filene Cooperative Association (FCA) in 1891 to benefit employees,

Open to all interested employees, the FCA was a tool with which employees could advocate for improved work conditions. The FCA elected an eighteen-member executive council, which could overturn any store policy through a two-thirds vote. If management vetoed the proposed rule change, a unanimous vote of the FCA membership could overturn the veto....

Functioning independently of the store management, the body had the power to challenge and reverse the decisions of store supervisors. Further, the Filene brothers assured the FCA that employees could vote in any manner without fear of management reprisal.[104]

In 1901 the Filene Cooperative Association included an arbitration committee which adjudicated all dismissal cases and disciplinary actions.

For its time, these actions were extremely progressive. Nevertheless they left a Fiat hierarchy in charge which split apart Wm. Filene Son's Co, traded it, and eventually it disappeared.

As Jack Quarter writes in *Beyond the Bottom Line*, as long as there is a boss around, he is *"resistive, and often desires to hold onto its authority. At the same time employees, conditioned to a powerless role in decision making, have difficulty expressing themselves, even when given the opportunity to do so."*[105]

To last, co-ownership *and* co-management need each other.

Braided Voices

The combination of co-ownership and co-management support each co-owner's voice. Every co-owner has the same right to speak up on a subject, any subject. Not as a shapeless mob, but as an aligned community.

Having listened to those who speak, the group will have a chance to align with a voice that represents *"the highest level of consciousness,"* to use Laloux' terminology or the highest *"psychic force"* as Mary Parker Follet put it 100 years earlier.[106] This is not a single voice, but the integration of all contributions made.

Their voices braid and the human voice and the melody of conversation makers the community dance and move forward.

Fiat Hierarchy

A Fiat hierarchy makes it impossible to co-manage or co-own a business. With a Fiat hierarchy in place, co-management is at best *temporary* or *lip service*. If you have a boss who can fire you, or demote, or otherwise punish you, you will hold back on what you say. Your ability to make decisions and take action will be very, very restricted.

Co-ownership opens the door to real novel innovation to come from anybody, not just a select few. If you start to implement it and it becomes obvious that it is not going to work, the co-owners working on it will know and pull the red flag. If it looks like it's going to work, the co-owners will probably make it better and get it out the door sooner.

A boss limits the level of consciousness that a group can attain because his voice is the only one that can be heard and, no matter what, employees must follow the boss' directions. We need a system that unblocks the group's *"capacity for independent action"* that doesn't depend on a benevolent boss. We need a system where everyone counts and there's no set limit to where the group can reach.

A Fiat boss can cancel any decision that a subordinate makes. So what if you and your peers spent hours interviewing a candidate and after a five minute conversation with the boss says, *"I don't think he'd be a good fit."* The boss made a decision and that's all you need to know.

Agile

The current state of Agile software development is the canonical example. The original idea was to have software developed by a complete, self-managed team. But even with the best intentions, it is impossible to sustain a self-managed team within a Fiat hierarchy. For example,

- The daily standup meeting turns into a reporting-to-the-boss-meeting not because the boss is a bad person but because *his job is to report up* the hierarchy.

- It doesn't matter that the Agile team discovered a major obstacle, you can't take it out of scope because sales promised that feature already, ...and who's going to tell the CEO?
- Delivering "value to our customer" plays second fiddle to everything else.
- There are a few pockets of co-managed Agile teams here and there, but they're very fragile. Mostly they revolve around an enlightened boss who is clever enough to hide it and protect it. Once the enlightened boss is out of the picture, the experiment ends, regardless of results.

The Fiat hierarchy values the perception of control above all else.

21th Century Commons

It would be great if we had a framework for building a Radical company. It would guide us as individuals, as teams, and as an organization. It would allow us to figure out if we are making progress or not. Well, the framework we describe below comes close.

Radical Framework

For the Radical Framework, we took inspiration from the work of political economist Elinor Ostrom, the first woman to win the Nobel Prize in Economics. Ostrom's award was based on her work with Commons, or as she called them *Common Pool Resources*.

She framed her findings as eight Core Design Principles,

1 Boundaries of users and resource are clear

2 Congruence between benefits and costs

3 Users had procedures for making own rules

4 Regular monitoring of users and resource condition

5 Graduated sanctions

6 Conflict resolution mechanism

7 Minimal recognition of rights by government

8 Nested enterprises

Ostrom's work showed that *"people in small, local communities managed shared natural resources, such as pastures, fishing waters, and forests"* and the successful ones agreed *"for how these are to be cared for and used in a way that is both economically and ecologically sustainable."*[107]

As we see it, Radical companies are the Commons of the twenty-first century.

Commons and Radical companies are managed by the people who embody them (co-management) and in both cases they dynamically share the benefit of their work (co-ownership).

Core Design Principles

Here's our take on Ostrom's *Core Design Principles* and how they apply to Radical companies,

#1. Clearly defined boundaries

Clear, explicit definition of 1) what determines who can be a member of a team or a company, 2) who has rights to extract wealth from the company, and 3) the company's constitutional framework that specifies what it is about.

This Core Design Principles applies both to the company as a whole, to each team, and to ensembles. Who is and is not a member is probably the most important criterion that needs to be made explicit.

At a company level, a member is anybody who contributes to its Foundation (**Impact**, **Purpose**, and **Mission**). If they end up contributing to the company, then they are co-owners. Their contribution is determined by other members.

Even a capital investor can be a co-owner if the investor helps, say, bring in new customers. She can also be a co-owner if she offers valuable advice given on her experience and skills.

There is no hiring, per se. Teams are responsible for recognizing contributions, or not. Again, these could be full-time members of the team or more casual contributors.

#2. Balanced contributions and benefits

The balance of contributions, recognition, and other rewards must be trusted as fair and equitable.

As Dr Paul Atkins, Prosocial, points out, *"Perceived fairness is essential for high group performance."*[108]

And not just people. The video below shows the capuchin monkey on the left vigorously objecting to his getting a (low worth) cucumber while his neighbor on the right gets a (high worth) grape *for doing the same task.*

[109]

They've run this experiment with dogs, birds, and chimpanzees with the same results.

For Radical companies, the insistence on transparency makes it possible to fully support this Core Design Principle. Any co-owner can figure if contributions and benefits are, to them, fairly balanced or not.

Contributions are relative to the group's alignment (*e.g.*, **Impact**, **Purpose**, **Mission**). It could be introducing a new practice or improving an existing one. Anything, with broad positive impact.

If you do something that moves our **Purpose** forward, you'd likely be recognized. The important thing is that the act and the reward be transparent and balanced. Capricious and arbitrary rewards is the kind of thing that happens more often than not in Fiat managed companies. The boss' favorite always gets applauded for even the simplest things, while the amazing deeds of others can easily be dissed because "*the boss doesn't like you.*"

For example, take budget allocation. The process for defining and allocating budgets has to be transparent and equitable. In a Fiat managed business, the boss' pet project gets the big budget while everybody else fights for the crumbs. In a Radical company, the budgeting process is in members' hands and it is transparent.

#3. Inclusive Decision Making

Anybody affected by a decision must participate in the process of making that decision.

As we interpret it, this is one of the earliest practices that we made explicit at Nearsoft: anybody impacted by a decision must participate in that decision in some way, shape, or form. This has worked well for us.

At Nearsoft it also meant that, for example, any group rule can be questioned and changed at any time. Here again, the important thing is the discussion. This includes getting ejected from a team. If you are thinking, "*but HR already does that,*" think again.

In Fiat businesses, HR is responsible first and foremost for shielding its top executives from lawsuits.[110] The HR Department is part of the bureaucratic control apparatus, *"with its emphasis on methodical, rational-legal rules for direction, hierarchical monitoring, and rewards for compliance."*[111]

So, when a boss wants to get rid of an employee, he dumps her on HR. Now that the decision has been made, HR's job is to dutifully inform said employee that she is going to be *"put on a plan,"* a euphemism for, *"you are going to get fired and we're going to do it all nice and legal so you can't sue us."*

In a Radical company, before somebody is ejected from a team, she would have gotten plenty of feedback from her immediate team and others on what's not working. This didn't happen consistently at Nearsoft, humans that we are, but when it does, the offending person listens to the feedback, applies as appropriate, or takes himself out of the team (although, in a few cases there was more of a push). Until I left, there were only three cases when people had to be formally 'liquidated.'

#4. Monitoring

People are responsible for and accountable to each other. Regular, formalized check-ins are essential to the health of a team. Reviews and feedback are valuable gifts.

In a Radical company, monitoring is pretty much shaped by what needs to be monitored. The dangers are, 1) doing it surreptitiously, and 2) doing it as a tool of control.

I used to always interpret *monitoring* as a controlling act. Time clocks, hidden cameras, tracking technology. But monitoring doesn't have to be malicious or punitive.

Monitoring is key to coordination. Teams come together to work on shared tasks (*"hold it up while I nail it"*) and interdependent tasks (*"let me know when you're finished nailing it, so I can paint it"*). Something as simple as asking *"Is this high enough?"* is a form of monitoring.

Instead of leaving it to chance, monitoring needs to be made explicit, *"Every Monday at 10:30 AM Pacific."*

The specifics are not important and will be different for every team and whatever needs to be monitored. These will change as the team and circumstances change.

Trust has nothing to do with monitoring. In particular, having a monitoring process doesn't mean that we don't trust each other; not having one does not mean that we trust each other unconditionally, either.

Monitoring is just another aspect of co-management.

My own tendency was to resist any form of monitoring, particularly with people I trust. *"Let me know if anything comes up."* But that doesn't work well enough. It puts too much of the onus on the individual to divine what, when, and how to solicit feedback. Monitoring is an *us* activity and one that we can't just dump on others.

Dr Paul Atkins, in PROSOCIAL, points out that to be successful, monitoring needs to be done consistently.

Rich Barlett of Loomio, a bossless organization, makes a similar observation about developing a regular rhythm.[112] In their view, the rhythm promotes accountability, focus, and agility.

#5. Graduating Sanctions

Misconduct must be dealt with gradually, with sanctions that range from the gentle to the harsh. Just as important is to deal with sanctions in a transparent and balanced way and to do so decisively and quickly.

Ostrom observed that Commons worked better when sanctions went from gentle and good natured to unequivocal. This is no different for Radical companies.

Define a process for dealing with misdeeds, no good comes out of ignoring bad deeds. No matter how little, the team must learn to point out any and all kinds of misconduct; people are usually pretty good at recognizing it, but voicing it is difficult, to put it mildly, because we often confuse feedback and criticism. Nevertheless, bringing them out and having a discussion about them is key. In fact, many times that's all it takes.

Whatever you do, moving quickly: letting the process stall is painful.

I've heard it said often enough that this is something that bosses do well and the rest of the people don't want to deal with it. Better for a boss to deal with the bad apple. From my own experience, bosses are generally worse at this than teams are. They ignore the misdeeds of their favorites, over-penalize the people they don't like, they don't often understand and leave the issues unresolved and festering. When they do act, it usually comes as a sudden rushing of somebody out the door. So, definitely no, bosses are *not* especially good at this. Worst, how the bosses handle this is opaque to everybody else. People hear the nervous murmuring in the hallways, but they don't really know what really happened and are left to make up their own stories.

Having a system of graduated sanctions is probably important, but, as Ostrom stated, just as important is to deal with sanctions in "*a transparent and balanced way and to do so decisively and quickly.*"

#6. Conflict management

In order to resolve conflicts effectively and inexpensively (both optionally and financially), recognizing and voicing conflicts is an essential skill.

Ostrom's original observation was about not jumping straight away to dragging neighbors through the legal system.[113]

However, for Radical companies, it is not just about resolving conflicts. Conflict has to be recognized and be brought out in the open before we can even talk about resolving it. Resolution is often not the hardest phase. More difficult than a resolution is getting people to point out the conflict and bring it out in the open. This going to be hard.

From our first breath, we are taught to ignore conflict, walk away from it, go around it and we never learn to deal with it effectively. The usual pattern is to put up with it and put up with it until you can't take it anymore, explode and walk away. It is more important to learn to say it out loud without exploding or walking away. Once the source of conflict is brought out to the open, its resolution becomes a matter of conversations.

For example, in the Nearsoft interview process, it sometimes happens that the candidate is clearly not aligned with our Values. When that happens we bring it out by plainly telling the candidate about our concerns. In my own experience doing interviews, I'll point out specific problems to the candidate and then we have a conversation that either resolves the issues on the spot or we talk about specific areas to improve for next time.

Every conflict is a chance to learn about us and about other members. Different people see the world differently, and resolving conflict is mostly a matter of aligning these differing views.

There are people who are a natural at handling conflict well and with elegance. Most of us need training and practice. All of us can master it.

For Radical companies then, this *Core Design Principle* points out how important it is to learn to deal with conflict. The ability to recognize, voice, and resolve conflict is a must-have skill.

#7. Co-ownership as right-to-manage

Co-management is an integral part of Radical companies, not the special characteristic of isolated teams. Co-ownership is what gives a Radical company the right to co-manage.

For Radical companies, this is a given.

Fiat managed businesses can transform to co-management and gain the right to co-manage.

K2K Emocionando in Bilbao, Spain helps businesses go through that transformation and has done it successfully many, many times. They are proof that it is possible for Fiat businesses to metamorphosize into co-managed businesses, but it does take conviction and courage.

As we've pointed out, co-management is fragile and temporary if it depends on a benevolent owner. Co-ownership is what gives a Radical company the right to co-manage.

#8. Polycentric governance

Radical companies are decentralized and as such are governed policentrically. They also touch and are touched by many other adjunct communities including parent companies, subsidiaries, customers, candidates, industry peers, and the civil communities they are part of. Ostrom observed that, *"Appropriation, provision, monitoring, enforcement, conflict resolution, and governance activities are organized in multiple layers of nested enterprises."* Ostrom was thinking of agencies that usually get involved with Common Pool Resources.

Ostrom originally called this principle *Nested Enterprises*. Later, Vincent Ostrom, her husband and economist, suggested that this *Core Design Principle* be renamed *Polycentric Governance*, the shared governance of interdependent peer nodes.

In fact, Radical companies themselves become policentrically governed as they grow. They're decentralized organizations, with many decision making centers that come and go fluidly, as conditions require. What holds them together as a company is their Explicit Alignment (*e.g.*, around **Impact**, **Purpose**, and **Missions**).

In addition, Radical companies also interact with their customers, industry peers, suppliers, candidates, and other communities they are part of.

Self-Assessment Tool

Based on the Ostrom Framework, we came up with this tool that a company can use to quickly assess itself against these design principles. The results give you a high level picture of the company's strengths and weaknesses. From there, you can figure out how to move the needle in one or more areas.

As a test, I did a quick seat of the pants assessment of Nearsoft (before the sale),

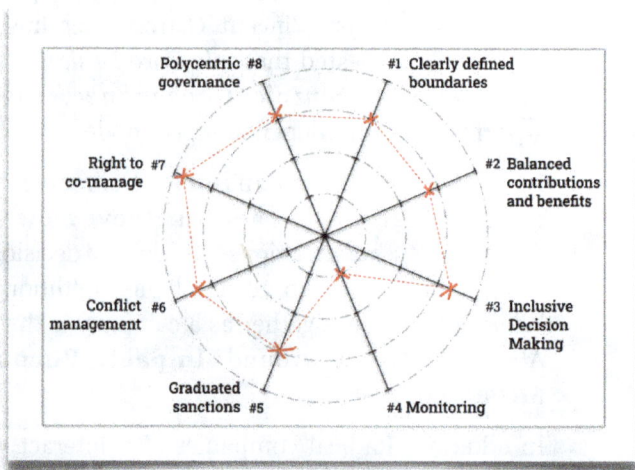

The results made it abundantly obvious that, in general, I felt that Nearsoft was weak when it came to Monitoring.

Productivity?

Early on some of our early clients would ask us how we tracked people to make sure that we *"were being productive."* Around the time we started, there were body shops that were very proud of the fact that they took a snapshot of people's screens every few seconds as proof that their people were working and prospects learned to ask us if we supported similar technology, but with a bit of prodding it was obvious that they also *knew* that this approach would be counterproductive.

Eventually we learned to explain,

- That we didn't do that

- Why we didn't do it

- Why they didn't want to work with businesses that relied on that type of sneaky behavior.

That usually was enough to deal with the question; and when it wasn't, it made it clear that the prospect and us were not a good match.

In any case, that's what monitoring meant to me: sneaky, intrusive, and punitive. It didn't occur to me then that monitoring is actually neutral. It doesn't have to be coercive and it doesn't have to lead to punishment. In fact, we monitor each other all the time, as when we look out for one another.

These days, we have a healthier view of monitoring at Nearsoft, but we have a lot of catch up to do.

Cultural Transformation

Moving away from a Fiat towards a Radical approach requires experimentation. Lots of it. In fact, the experimentation never ends. A culture emerges as people interact around those experiments. You can't transform a company's culture by lecturing, bringing outside experts, or turning to online courses. It is an honest-to-goodness paradigm shift and it is not easy to do.

The full transformation is two-fold: from Fiat ownership to co-ownership and from Fiat management to co-management. For a sustained transformation you need both.

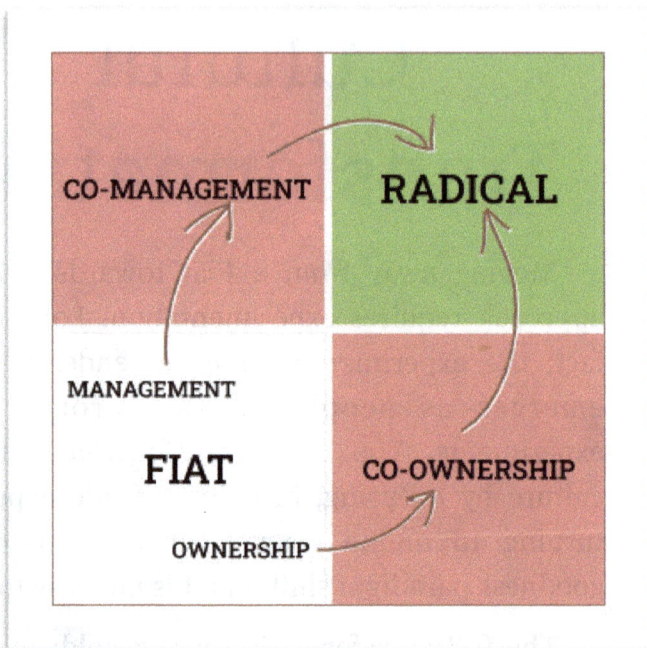

Co-management is enough to get people excited. For example, the various forms of Open Books Management have demonstrated that just knowing about the finances of a company is enough to get people engaged. This is also why there's so much excitement about self-management today. What's missing, and it's absolutely required for the long term, is decentralized ownership.

Every company is different. There is no pre-packaged solution that will work for your company. And what works today won't necessarily work tomorrow. From my own experience, the way that Nearsoft operates today would have been overkill for the Nearsoft of years ago and vice versa.

In fact, every time we hire a new person, the company changes. You never know who is going to have a big impact, or when. I have been surprised by the impact some people have made, even some I originally thought were too green to make a difference.

We need to embrace experimentation and make learning a foundation of company culture. *Failure* is not failure unless you don't learn from it.

> **Zulema Salinas**
> @Zulema184
>
> Replying to @Ridruejita
>
> Todo cuenta al final. De lo malo se aprende y de lo bueno tomamos el aliento para seguir. Me siento afortunada. Un abrazo 🤗 😘
>
> Translate Tweet
>
> 4:02 AM · Aug 19, 2020 · Twitter Web App

114

Everything counts when it is all said and done. From the bad, you learn and from the good we get inspiration to continue. I feel fortunate. Hugs.

In order to fully become an co-owner, you have to also become a fully functioning adult and grow out of your "*good employee*" habits.

The Good Employee

> ... even the knowledge and full conviction of a truth will not always immediately conquer inveterate habits and prejudices.
>
> — *Viktor Frankl, Man's Search for Meaning*

- The good employee appears docile, does as he's told, and never puts his boss in a bad light.
- Is OK when one of his bosses appropriates her ideas and presents them as his.
- Laughs at his bosses' jokes (wether or not he finds them funny).
- Always delivers on time, but if she can't, he is ready to explain why the delay is somebody else's fault.
- An ambitious employee is very alert to any criticism and is quick to rebut it. Any comment short of positive is a criticism and may block his from moving up the ladder.

- A hard-working employee is always busy. Always supports his boss in emails and chat messages. Always writes down boss-friendly things (*i.e.*, because the boss will somehow find them and read them).
- A good boss is a good employee to his boss. And, of course, he expects his people to be good employees to him.

These are some of the habits and prejudices that we all pick up as we grow up in a Fiat world. Be obedient and don't make waves that will send you to the Principal's office.

We need to outgrow these habits as we transform into full adults. I know that this is possible with the minimum of support and encouragement from the team, as I've seen at Nearsoft.

We Know Nothing

Before embarking on a cultural transformation, it'd be good to know what we really know. And we know little to nothing about alternatives to the Fiat world we live in. All we know today is the Fiat model that has come together over a relatively long time and we really know nothing of what a different world would look and work like.

There are a bunch of studies about *"the nature of people,"* but they really are about *"the nature of* people ***who were born and grew up in the Fiat system***.*"* We cannot learn much about living on dry land by studying fish.

Take, for example, Robert Kegan's *Socialized Mind*.[115] According to Kegan, a psychologist and author, the transformation from what he calls the *Socialized Mind* to the *Self-Transforming Mind* doesn't start until we are in our 40s. But we suspect that it's a chicken-and-egg situation: it looks that way because that's what we are taught throughout our lives. He's discovered a novel pattern in the data and that's great, but that data is about *the Fiat system* we live in, not about the nature of people.

In the 1940s, *"Education leaders presumed that 60% or more of all public school students lacked the intellectual capability for college work or even for skilled occupations."*[116] They didn't make up the data, they reported on what they found back then. But what was true in the 1940s is laughable today.

The Fiat paradigm teaches us to remain dependent on the people above us, on those more powerful, and so Kegan's finding is not surprising. We suspect that as we get away from the Fiat paradigm, people will start to develop into self-transforming adults earlier and earlier. People will shake their heads that we ever believed them incapable of developing as full adults before the age of 40.

More than likely, I think we will find that the socialized mind is *always* there and so is the self-transforming mind.[117] Otherwise we would have perished as a species.

When we started Nearsoft, we were told over and over that co-management would not work. *"Where are you going to find enough people who can work without a manager? It's going to stunt your growth!"* In the history of Nearsoft, from 2007 until the time of this writing, only three people have left the company because of *"not enough* (Fiat) *structure."* Over 450 Nearsoftians have done fine. It turns out that the people who take well to being treated as adults are neither special nor rare.

What this tells us is that we know nothing about what the world will look like as we move away from the Fiat paradigm.

Keep this in mind as you get well-intentioned advice from those *in the know*.

Power Distance

In the early 1970s, Geert Hofstede came up with his *Cultural Dimensions Theory* based on his worldwide survey of (old) IBM employees. Of the original five dimensions, Power Distance is, to us, the most key,

> Power Distance... the extent to which the less powerful members of organizations and institutions *accept and expect* that power is distributed unequally. It suggests that a society's level of inequality is endorsed by the followers as much as by the leaders. ...[118] (emphasis added)

In other words, it is not the power *they take*, but the power *we give* them. That was quite a revelation to me when I first read about it!

The lesson then is that we must learn to not give our power away so readily. This is feasible at a local level, and there's nothing more local than the workplace (*i.e.*, even in multinationals businesses).

National biases and norms don't disappear, but they can be modulated. I've seen this at work at Nearsoft. At a Power Distance score of 81, Mexico is a hierarchical society—but not so inside Nearsoft. People learn from other people.

Nearsoft's Orientation program went from a hello and a handshake, to two weeks, and then six weeks. It's been effective at getting new people to recognize the habits they bring with them and then to start to move away from them and replace them with healthier habits (*e.g.*, speak up, self-direct, and let yourself be seen, rather than sulk and complain in the hallways). This Orientation gives a taste of what working at Nearsoft is like, but the transformation is not immediate. There is a lot to unlearn.

According to Pablo Aretxabala, an ex-member of K2K Emocionando, getting started on the path of co-management takes a couple of months, but "*to consolidate the new mindset, behavior, and habits may take two or three years.*"[119]

Self-Emancipation

Whenever the topic of co-ownership and co-management comes up, the next question is *"how can I do it?"* And the answer is that it is going to be difficult. Very exciting and hugely beneficial, but not a walk in the park for either startups or established businesses.

There are many companies that are experimenting with aspects of it, including Liqueed and Happyforce in Spain, 10Pines, Basetis, and Manas in Argentina, UruIt in Uruguay, Pressto in Peru, Tegu in Honduras, Grupo Cygnus in Chile, and Vagas and Grupo Anga in Brazil, Semillas del Caribe, Grupo Qualia, and VkusVill in Russia.[120]

Since 2007, *K2K Emocionando* in Northern Spain has made a business out of helping Fiat businesses convert to co-management, including some aspects of co-ownership. Before they commit to taking on a client, the business owners have to unanimously sign an agreement to keep their hands-off operations and share the company's numbers with the workers. The owners and the workers agree to share profits and risks, but it is not quite co-ownership because the equity remains in the hands of the Fiat owners (*e.g.*, they can sell the company at any time). Nevertheless, K2K has shown that there is a repeatable process to transform established Fiat *business* into near-Radical *companies*.

As people practice co-management and deconstruct the Fiat house of cards, they also peel off the internal Fiat shackles that we all carry around with us.

Nevertheless, converting to co-ownership is going to be a huge hump to get over that only the most daring will attempt.

Crisis as Opportunity

Established businesses are more likely to try anything at a time of crisis. Even a transformation to co-management.

That was the case at SEMCO, a crisis that caused its owner, Ricardo Semler, to get their seminal transformation started. As he wrote in Maverick, the transformation helped them get out from under the crisis.

Similarly, at Yash Papers, in India, there was a crisis that kicked off the company's transformation. In 1999, a curfew kept the bosses from getting to the factory, so the workers self-organized, got supplies on credit and had a record production. The founder, KK Jhunjhunwala, had read Semler's Maverick and he was all for experimenting with co-management. Later, his son, Ved Krishna, kept it up when he took over the company. In 2012, Ved had his own personal crisis. He didn't waste this combined crisis, either. He came up with a new, Earth-friendly product line and doubled down on co-management.

By the way, what happened at Yash shows that co-management can work anywhere in the world. Even, "in a culture where hierarchy is very strongly ingrained."[121] With the help of consultants Pradeep Chakravarthy[122] and Suresh Pandit,[123] they reached back to India's roots and its temple system, when self-governance was alive and well in India. They've adapted these practices to work at Yash and they are well out from under the crisis.

A crisis is an opportunity to get started on the Radical journey. The combination of co-management and co-ownership can help a company's financial performance by increasing profits, reducing costs (e.g., turnover). The tradeoff is accepting a loss of the perception of control, but a company in crisis is obviously not under control. If there's one thing that Fiat owners understand is that getting something for nothing is good and if it leads out of the crisis, it's even better.

People at the Center

People as Resources

Fiat businesses don't prioritize people at all. For Fiat businesses, power and the perception of control are most important. So are the rules. And so are the deadlines, as arbitrary as they might be. But, oh, yeah, be nice.

When Nearsoft was a small company of less than 10 people it was easy enough to prioritize people and put them at the center. Indeed, most startups are people-centered when the team is small, there is a lot of uncertainty, and they are aligned to a common vision. Then capital investment happens and all that goes down the Fiat drain and making money takes the top spot,

Our revenue is below target? Fire enough resources to bring back our capital gains.

Rent is going up? Pack resources closer together—but leave the corner offices untouched.

But as Angel investor Dr Alicia Castillo would say, *"humans are not resources."*

People are living, breathing social animals. Our work has to make sense to us and we need to know, *"why do we have to do X instead of Y?"* We need to understand to contribute, *"maybe we should be working on Z?"* The desire to belong to a group is built into our DNA, literally.

None of this was clear to us as we built Nearsoft, it just felt right to put people at the center. By doing what was right for people we created the conditions for what became a people-centered culture, with less of the fear that is so ingrained in Fiat businesses. We treated everybody as adults, not as 'clients' or 'employees,' and this created value for us and our clients from day one.

Focusing on people and treating each other as adults was an early expression of where Nearsoft was headed.

Bound by Iron Bars

> Our bureaucratic rules ultimately confine us as solidly as if we were in a cage bound by iron bars.
>
> — *James Barker, Tightening the Iron Cage*[124]

Control is embodied in Fiat bureaucracies. Arbitrary as they may be, bureaucratic rules can be more effective than an armed guard. We just have to follow the rules and we are all treated by the same rules.

Richard Edwards, an economist, says, "... *the great contradiction in bureaucratic control is its implicit tyranny. Workers are treated fairly within the rules, but they have no say in establishing the rules.*"[125] These rules become an invisible iron cage.

Professor Gary Hamel and coauthor Michele Zanini wrote a whole book on bureaucracy and they came to the conclusion that we need an alternative, "*bureaucracy was invented by human beings and now it's up to us to invent something better.*"[126] Except every one of our habits keeps us from breaking out of the iron cage and reaching out for something better. Left to their old habits, there's a good chance that a team becomes its worst boss and becomes emotionally attached to its rules and then coerces members to adapt to these rules. This is what professor James Barker calls *concertive control.*

One possible way to avoid this kind of iron cage is to review the team's rules and norms on a regular basis. For example, when a new person joins the team, write down the team's rules and norms individually on pieces of paper and then drop them all in the trash can.

Now you have a clean slate!

Then, take each rule out of the trash, one at a time, and review it. Each rule either earns its place back on the slate or it stays in the trash. Even if new members don't ask any challenging questions (*e.g.*, because they won't yet feel safe enough), the exercise of questioning their own rules *shows* the new folks that 1) we are not attached to the rules we made up in the past, and 2) we have a new team with you in it and we may need new rules.

Structures, Agreements, and Norms

> ... conservatives believe that people need external structures or constraints in order to behave well, cooperate, and thrive.
>
> — *Jonathan Haidt, The Righteous Mind*[127]

Radical companies are based on structures, agreements, and norms, just like Fiat businesses. The *fundamental* difference is that these structures, agreements, and norms are created by the very people affected by them, not created externally nor handed down by imperial bosses. They are dynamic and adapt to emerging conditions and help the group *"behave well, cooperate, and thrive"* more effectively than arbitrary orders from on high.

But be careful; if they become immutable dogma, they will limit your ability to cooperate and prevent your ability to thrive.

A Joyful Place

> If people are laughing, they are learning. True learning is a joy because it is an act of creation.
>
> — *Tyson Yunkaporta, Sand Talk*[128]

Never forget that this is all about people. Companies are but a group of people who are aligned and experiment together and they get joy from the journey.

Richard Sheridan, an entrepreneur and author of Joy, Inc, is not shy about saying that he co-founded *Menlo Innovations*, a co-managed company, for selfish reasons. *"I desperately wanted to work in a joyful place with joyful people achieving joyful outcomes. I wanted to have fun at work while producing wonderful results within a sustainable business."*[129] We very much recognize with wanting to create a joyful place to do work we love, a place of "... *affective relations, sensuality, playing, laughing, loving."*[130]

One of the big advantages of *not* having a Fiat hierarchy is that you can make it about what's good and healthy for people as Richard and his co-workers did. Yes, a company has to be financially sustainable, but don't let an obsession with arbitrary targets take precedence over people's joy.

Beware that these targets may be positioned as *"crushing the competition"* or *"winning."* You can recognize these decisions when they are,

- Arbitrary
- Focused on financial targets only
- Made by a handful of owners.
- Dehumanize the workplace.

Whatever you do, a company should be a source of joy. A space where people can bring their whole selves to work, warts and all. This is about making work just another aspect of one's life, not just a miserable survival mechanism.

The Future of... Everything?

Making an Impact

Our existing businesses are broken because Fiat organizations prioritize control and obedience over everything else. You have likely seen the data from Gallup,[131] ADP,[132] and others. The results speak for themselves: most people are disengaged. They're miserable or numb. We think it's time to flip the script and view our organizations through a people lens rather than a simplistic financial one.

Imagine a truly people-centric culture, a workplace where people are valued and have a strong sense of belonging. Where they are surrounded by people that encourage each other to find meaning in their work and in all they do. And where there are no bosses demanding "*more, more* and preventing this from happening," This kind of world has already sparked the imagination of many who are working on making it happen.

Just look at all the different approaches to the so-called *Future of Work* out there, with more popping up every day. They are all valid reactions to a singular problem: our businesses are broken and they break people.

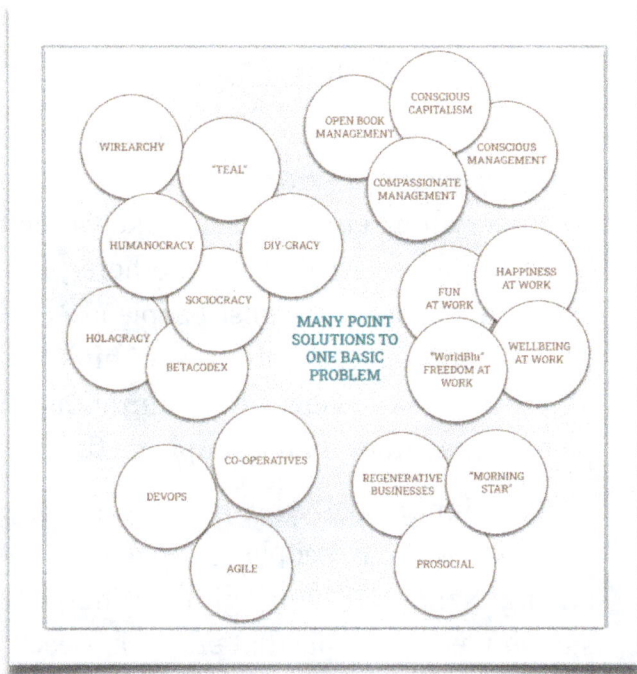

Doug Kirkpatrick has been a co-management practitioner for a very long time. He was part of the team that kicked off The Morning Star Company. He is also an author[133] and the closest thing to a philosopher of the co-management space. Trying to keep track of the field, he created a

Periodic Table[134] of all the different approaches, governance, frameworks, tools, media, associations, networks, conferences, and technologies. He even included what he calls *poets laureate* of the Future of Work, including Dee Hock, Peter Koestenbaum, Peter Drucker, Edgar Schein, Tom Peters, Gary Hamel, Fernando Flores, David Whyte, and Pim de Morree and Joost Minnaar (to which we would add Mary Parker Follet, and Ricardo Semler).

In spite of this, businesses continue to be broken and tactical solutions are not making a significant dent. Economist Umair Haque captures the feeling: *"Try as we might to embrace ethics, toe the line of responsibility, and accept fuzzy, vague notions of good citizenship, they seem ever in conflict with the sharp, cold edge of business."*[135]

Changing the System

A whole Future of Work industry has emerged. Books, blogs, podcasts, videos, courses, certifications, as well as experts, consultants, and self-proclaimed gurus. You can be happy, have fun at work. You can empower your people. You can learn about the five, eight, or 20 myths about self-management and how to make self-management work in five easy steps.

Some come as packaged solutions. But as professor, consultant, and author Gary Hamel puts it, *"I don't think that there's a single model that's even close to a one-size-fits all."*[136] It sounds appealing for our Fiat mind to have a ready-made recipe, but the right co-management formulation for any group of people can emerge only from experimentation by the people who are going to live it.

Alternatives

This reflects a broad hunger for alternatives to Fiat management. A good example of this is the popularity of the book *Reinventing Organizations* written by consultant Frederic Laloux. *Evolutionary Teal* is his label for organizations that fully support the autonomy of its members.

According to Laloux, *Teal* is not a destination, *"I suggest that leaders don't try to engage their organization saying, 'we'll become a Teal organization.'"*[137]

Regardless of that comment, people have been inspired want to see more of it in practice, and so there is a fledgling organic movement behind it now.

None of these approaches deal with what we consider the fundamental problem: ownership.[138] The problem, as we see it, is that we can't fix the Fiat system by tweaking it while leaving Fiat ownership in place. The system has to change. *"Changing the system might be even less work than pouring water on today's tactical emergency."*[139]

Part III

Our Radical Company

All Together Now

We want to see a world where people matter and are at the center of everything we do. To us, that's worth putting energy into. It's your turn now.

Go find others who are crazy enough to embark on this Radical journey with you. There are going to be a thousand things to do. This means that you will have to get good at running a thousand experiments at once.

The temptation is going to be there to fall back on Fiat habits. In fact, you will fall back on those habits and won't even notice because that's what you know. The challenge is to develop the sensitivity to question and recognize when you are drifting back to Fiat habits and to bring forth the courage to experiment with an unproven, people centered process.

Below are a few practices to help you get started, but be ready to experiment and replace them with whatever works best for you.

On Your Marks...

Let's start a shiny, brand new, Radical company!

I had a great idea in the shower this morning, but... wait... what kind of Impact is our new company going to have in the world? What would we be doing this for? And why would anybody want to do this with us, what is our Purpose?

Our Radical company is going to be rooted in our need to do things that mean something. Meaning and belonging aren't just words, they reflect how it affects us and how we engage. We have to create a meaningful space for others to engage and contribute in a way that makes sense to us all and gives us an identity as a community.

Ready, Set, Go!

Our Radical company is going to be co-owned and co-managed from the get-go, of course. That doesn't mean that I'll ignore the experience I've gained at Nearsoft all these years; we even have to considered Jose's and Adrian's suggestions.

But we will not impose our best (Fiat) practices on our new company. We'll try to tone it down, but it is going to be difficult for us to hold back because the best practices habit is hard to shake.

Obviously, our new company won't have an imposed hierarchy or bosses with grandiose titles. But that doesn't mean that we won't have a way to align with each other and form a coherent teams. In Fiat organizations, the boss determines what alignment there is to be had. Directly or indirectly, he sets the direction, the goals, assignments, and deadlines. He even decides what tools and vendors to use. In a Radical organization, you and I and every other contributor will be responsible for defining all that.

To belong in a team is to be aligned with it. Without alignment we are either isolated or simply going along with the team.[140] Full, warm participation in a caring communities starts with being aligned. Teams don't have to hug and kiss all the time to function, but they do have to develop affection for each other and appreciation for each other's contributions. If you are chronically just putting up with somebody in your group because you have to, then you two are not really a team.

So, let's leverage our principles, commitments, and practices to create our company.

The Radical Kitchen

Our new company would look more like an experimental kitchen, always cooking up new recipes, always making messes, and cleaning up better than before. There's no recipe that works in every instance and we are always trying new, better ones.

What worked for Nearsoft 10 years ago would not work today and vice versa. In 2007, we were eight people at Nearsoft. As of this writing, we are just well over 450 people and growing. We have no idea what will work for us next year and beyond.

> Caminante, no hay camino, se hace camino al andar.
>
> — *Antonio Machado*
>
> Wanderer there is no path, you make the path as you walk

Once we really get that we create our own path as we move forward, we'll be well on the way towards creating our own futures. Experiment like it is never going to end (because it's not).

To Each Their Own

The basic assumption of co-ownership is that a company's value is forever changing. As its revenue goes up or down, its value changes. Every time somebody joins or leaves, its value changes, too. Customers come and customers go and every time that happens, its value changes. Recognized contributions change frequently and as they change, their value change. And so will ownership.

At the very start, when there's merely a handful of people kicking a company off the ground, a simple, formulaic methodology for assigning ownership may work. But that only clunks along for ye long. Later, as the team gets bigger and things get more complex, you'll need a more robust method of distributing and accounting for ownership.

Slicing Pie

As we researched the concept of co-ownership and its related practices, we looked at *Slicing*

Pie.[141] According to Mike Moyer, inventor of *Slicing Pie, "the beauty of this thing... is your ability to start working with someone immediately."*

Impossible to Figure Out

Moyer is clear that at the start, the value of the company is not baked. As Moyer points out, trying to guess the value of a new company is a losing proposition. *"We don't know how much we're worth. We know that it's impossible to figure out this number, yet people try to do it all the time."*[142] Then capital investors get involved and force a valuation.

Valuations are a combination of fantasy and desperation. The investor supplies the fantasy, *"I'll give you $1M for 25% of the company."* By waving its magic wand, the investor has now declared that your company is worth $4M dollars! The desperation is supplied by the entrepreneur: if she thinks that the investors offer is too low but she's desperate enough for a capital infusion, then she'll take it, she'll buy into the fantasy.

But how does anybody know what the company is going to be worth in the future? What if the company grows to $1B in revenue? Does the fellow who invested $1M still owns 25% of the company no matter how large it gets? And, what about the people who did the work to turn the $1M into a $1B? what about the so-called employees? *"They got paid!"*

The value of a company is also *"impossible to figure out"* even after capital investors get involved. In the co-ownership model the pie never bakes.

The Pie Keeps Growing

The *Slicing Pie* rules are aimed at small, pre-investment teams. During a lecture at Stanford, Moyer said that *"when you go to your VC, ... your real money investor ... we're not playing by [the Slicing Pie] rules anymore, we're playing by regular business rules."*[143]

To be clear, a capital infusion can be very valuable. Besides the money itself, it signals that the company has become tangible enough for outsiders to bet on it. The investment is very welcome and celebrated in Radical companies, too. However, in the Radical case a *financial* investment does not grant investors any powers beyond a right to a *financial* reward.

In the Fiat model, capital takes over all financial and strategic decisions and relegates everybody to, at best, a financial beneficiary role. Whether they keep the founders around or they bring in their own CEO, the Fiat owners are in charge.

The Radical ownership model flips this situation on its head: capital is the financial beneficiary and members retain the power to make financial, strategic, and operational decisions. If changes are needed, that's up to the people who embody the company, not to the capital investors (*i.e.*, they can't fire the CEO, because there isn't one).

According to Moyer, "*Equity in a startup company is the risk that you are not going to get paid. Equity in an established company... it's more of an incentive, a bonus...*"[144] He is describing what is normal today in our Fiat world: if you are not taking a capital risk, then you are just acquired labor, a mere employee, and perhaps a bonus.

We find it mind-blowing that the same people who embrace the idea that ownership is an incentive for them can then turn around and declare that a fixed salary is plenty for everybody else. If ownership is a motivator for founders and investors, then why wouldn't it be just as strong a motivator for everyone in the team? *"Well, yes, you have to give them some equity, but keep them out making real decisions."*

The assumption is that once *"real money"* makes a bet, employees can just execute according to the plan. Creativity and commitment is no longer important. *"We just need people who can take orders and follow the plan."* This is the very mindset that is holding back our economies and making us all miserable and disengaged.

On the other hand, the co-ownership approach assumes that the plan is never perfect and it takes fully engaged and committed people to make a business thrive and grow. Co-ownership is the disrupting force that's improves people's wellbeing and is going to make our companies thrive financially beyond anything we've seen so far.

Valuing the Intangible

One of the things that *Slicing Pie* touches upon is how to get the founders and other early people a bigger slice of the pie. Moyer calls that *calibrating or partitioning the pie*,

> ... early Grunts* can 'harvest' some of the value they have created by calibrating the theoretical value to a higher number. The new value becomes the base against which they (and new Grunts entering the herd) will earn additional pie. Care must be taken to ensure that the new, calibrated amount does not overestimate what the actual value of the company will eventually be [and who knows what that is?]. If it does, the Grunts will be unhappy. As an alternative to calibration, the Grunts can 'partition' off part of the pie and split up the rest. Their partitioned percentage remains fixed while the rest changes based on inputs from the herd.[145]

*Ignore the *grunt* and *herd* terminology, please.

What Moyer is talking about is valuing the intangible. What is the original idea for the company worth? What about the many pivots that the founders went through before the company found its market? We can see how people who feel they've made a breakthrough would want to reward themselves. I sure did. This kind of accomplishment is cathartic, an experience that changes everyone involved.

Contributions need to be recognized in a tangible way, but *calibration* and *partitioning* are ham-fisted suggestions. His mention of *theoretical value* and his advice to *"not overestimate what the actual value of the company will eventually be"* go against Moyer's own *"impossible to figure out"* observation.

Elsewhere in this book, we consider different ways to recognize the founders' contribution, including financially (*i.e.*, once there is something to divvy up).

Radical Compensation

Compensation, including salary, has traditionally been treated as a function of performance (?), at least in theory. It feels awfully reminiscent of the allowance that kids get from their parents.

But salary is not an allowance or tied to individual performance. Salary is a form of wealth extraction. For sure, salary is limited by the performance of the whole business, but trying to pin it on one person is misguided, ineffective, and counterproductive.

Haier, a Chinese business that has become the poster child of self-management lately, has tried several compensation models. Their latest experiment is what they call their Customer Paid Salary System.[146] Although we don't find the approach transformational, it is an attempt at breaking out of the fixed salary model.

An example of disintermediated salaries is Manas, a small Argentinian software development company. On their own, they came up with a scheme very similar to the Rosedale Distribution. Founder Nicolas di Tada explains that "... *the only thing this system does is to compute in a short time the* optimal compensation scheme between team members... through a *distributed, uniform and disintermediated process.*"[147]

The first time I heard about self-set salaries was in 2007 while reading Maverick. Currently, several companies are using various forms of decentralized salaries, including BvdV, Finext, Hanno, Incentro, Makers Academy, The Morning Star, Smarkets,[148] Ragnarson,[149] Liqueed, Happyforce, 10Pines, Basetis, and Manas.[150] Unfortunately, at Nearsoft we got stuck in the Fiat way of assigning salaries and have not made any serious experiments to change this.

Different types of wealth extraction, including salaries, can be practiced at the same time. There doesn't have to be a one-and-only way of doing it— that is Fiat thinking. You'll need to experiment with different approaches.

Below are a handful of ideas to get you started, but there are many other alternatives around this topic and we hope that more will come up.

The Salary Offer

How can we determine a starting salary for new people? This is pretty difficult, actually.

The Fiat way is pretty straightforward. Tell me how much you made at your previous job and I'll offer a bit more, but not too much. And so on. This kind of competition leaves a bad aftertaste.

In the Radical case, once we are ready to invite her to join, let her figure out a salary that works for her and the company. She already is a de facto member and with the help of other co-owners, she can identify people who are most like her. Those people can even suggest others who would be even more akin to her in skills, experience, etc. She could then get together with her future peers and figure out a starting salary for her.

This can actually go much faster than the traditional Fiat way. The right people get involved from the beginning and get to know each other, build trust, and figure out this puzzle together. No negotiation necessary and no bad aftertaste.

Predictable Recurring Income (PRI)

When you really think about it, salary is a Fiat tool. Employees get income predictability in exchange for obedience: follow orders and get a paycheck.

Salaries, such as they are today, do not quite fit in the Radical context. In fact, when the subject first came up, I thought messing with salaries was wrong-headed. After a lot of back and forth, this is what we came up with,

- Each member determines their Predictable Recurring Income (PRI). This is what they need to take home every month. Some people will start too high and others will start too low, but we will all learn over time.

- For the company, along with expenses, loan repayment, and other fixed expenses, the sum of all PRIs determines what for simplicity we'll call the company's breakeven point.

- Every month, the company pays its bills and all PRIs and what's left is distributed as Earned Dividends according to each person's RAD allocations. This is the happy path.

- When revenue doesn't cover the breakeven point, a PRI Account for each member provides predictability. As a company we take on a debt obligation in exchange for an investment into this fund. Then, as needed, money flows out of the PRI Account to cover a member's full PRI.

- Each co-owner is responsible for her PRI Account and has to pay back what they got out of it. Most likely, this will be paid back out of Earned Dividends once revenue goes above breakeven, but this is something you'd have to experiment with.

- In the worst case, if the company goes belly up, then if the PRI Account was funded with investment money, there's no debt to be paid back. If it was funded with a loan, then people with unpaid balances have to make good on that loan.

This is one way of dealing with the Radical equivalent of salaries. Experiment and figure out what works for you.

Not Just for Startups

Something like the PRI scheme is not limited to new companies. It would also work when an organization is faced with a financial crisis. When revenue plummets, some co-owners will be able to handle it financially, and some won't. Their declared PRIs will tell.

It would also work for individual situations, when co-owners go through major, unexpected changes in their lives. Just imagine the surprise of having quintuplets—that would change anybody's PRI, big time. The five-time parent could raise her PRI, at least for a while.

There is also the not-so-happy situation where a company cannot sustain its PRI. Members are drawing most or all of their PRI from their PRI Accounts and there's little chance that the company can ever reach breakeven. In that case, the team may have to revisit the PRI levels and do something about the situation. Whatever the case, PRIs are not a magic wand to wish away hard times or difficult decisions.

The PRI scheme is transparent and decentralized. It affords everybody more agency, makes dealing with hard times a lot less stressful, and can lead to better decisions. Also, the fact that it gives everybody a chance to learn to handle risk will make our companies, and our economies, more resilient.

Splitting the Atom

At first we thought that this section's title was a bit too dramatic, but splitting power from capital may be a lot more difficult than splitting the atom. The idea that power and capital are one thing is pretty old, and many Fiat owners are going to feel that co-ownership robs them of... something.

And it kind of does. It eliminates the bosses governance power. It doesn't mess around with their money or their ability to contribute.

On the other hand, separating power from capital is what the financial markets already do: when you buy common stock in the stock markets you don't get any form of operational or strategic control. None. You bought the stock on the bet that you can later sell it at a higher price. In the meantime, you have no say in how the business is run, who is in charge, or what the company's market strategy should be. So long as its stock price is going up, you are supposed to be as happy as a pig in mud. If something bothers you about the business, your only practical option is to sell its stock.

As an investor in a Radical company you get a *predictable* financial return. And it does not prevent you from becoming a co-owner contributing to the company in other ways.

Fiat Ownership

Traditional ownership is about having control over a business. In Fiat owned businesses the Board of Directors[169] is the top owner. Directors are supposed to be fiduciaries who act "*in the interest of*" all shareholders.

Among other things, the Board is responsible for,

- Attesting the business' performance to other shareholders.

- Broad governance policies.

- Making sure there's enough financing to meet goals.

- Approving annual budgets.

- Setting compensation for execs, the top bosses.

- How much to pay as dividends, if any.

- Ownership distribution (*e.g.,* options and stock grants).

- Fate of the company (*e.g.,* selling all or part of it).

The Directors must get the company to be finally profitable; otherwise they risk getting sued. Everything else is secondary, including the impact on employees.

Real Contributions

In the Fiat model, investors get a seat on the Board or some other form of power over operations. When a Radical company accepts a capital infusion, it takes on a financial obligation but it doesn't assign it any other special powers,

- Capital does not automatically force a valuation.

- Ownership continues to be dynamically allocated by the co-owners as the company grows.

- Capital does not beget operational power. In particular, it does not include the power to arbitrarily fire the non-existent CEO.

In reality, when a company is heading off the rails, the people who show up to work every day will know about it well before the Board even hears about it. This information will eventually get to the Board; emphasis on eventually. Co-owners of a Radical company are more likely to move to fix this situation earlier, more decisively, and in a more nuanced way than a traditional Board. *Their* business is at stake, and more importantly, *their* Impact, *their* Purpose, and *their* Missions are at risk. *Their lives* are on the line. They are in a better position to pass judgement, make the right decision, and find a healthy way to address it.

In a Radical company there is nothing preventing a Radical investor from becoming part of the team, too. It may be that an investor has the best, most balanced suggestions and people follow it. Her experience, not the girth of her investment, leads the way and the company benefits from it.

Utterly Ridiculous

Another reason why splitting power from capital is going to be difficult is because this whole Radical thing will sound foreign to many people, not just Fiat owners. For example,

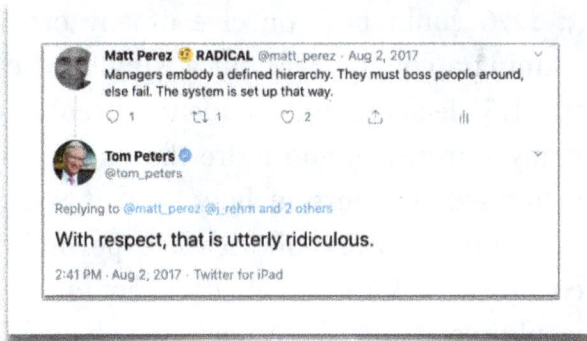

> **Matt Perez 🔴 RADICAL** @matt_perez · Aug 2, 2017
> Managers embody a defined hierarchy. They must boss people around, else fail. The system is set up that way.
>
> ○ 1　　　↻ 1　　　♡ 2　　　△　　　⏹
>
> **Tom Peters** ✓
> @tom_peters
>
> Replying to @matt_perez @j_rehm and 2 others
>
> **With respect, that is utterly ridiculous.**
>
> 2:41 PM · Aug 2, 2017 · Twitter for iPad

Peters has consistently and enthusiastically celebrated the excellence that people are capable of bringing to the table. Where we part ways with Peters is in putting the burden completely on the individual when the problem really is with the way businesses operate.

It's the barrel, not the apples.

Individual heroics will always run up against what's allowed by the Fiat system. By all means, individuals should aim for excellence and heed the direction that Peters points to. But they don't have a chance to make a lasting impact unless we create companies where *everybody* can pursue excellence, not just managers.

Understandably, it is difficult to conceive of any other way of organizing a company other than the Fiat way. The same way that most people on July

3, 1776 could not conceive of any other way of running a country without a King. And even after the US declared independence from George III, many Europeans and more than a few Americans continued to question how soon it was going to take before the American experiment would collapse. Back then, nobody knew for certain if it would work, but the American Colonies had been experimenting quite a bit with different flavors of governance.

A Strong Hand

Unfortunately, the *"you need a strong hand"* feeling has persisted. Even in the late 1960s, I had a very dear family member who believed that Generalísimo Franco was good for Spain. *"That country needs a strong man to lead it to prosperity."* Never mind that Franco was a dictator and had an authoritarian choke on Spain, very much like the one we had left behind in Cuba.

The French Revolution and its quick retreat to Napoleon's authoritarian rule gave fuel to the strong hand camp. Edmund Burke, Thomas Paine's nemesis, bemoaned that *"when the old feudal and chivalrous spirit of fealty... shall be extinct in the minds of men, plots and assassinations will be anticipated by preventive murder and preventive confiscation..."*[152] It sounds like 'without a boss' there will be chaos and mayhem at work. Where would employees get their direction from? When will they have time to do real work? How else would you make sure that the lazy employees are working hard to make the owner wealthier?

It only follows that any talk of moving away from the Fiat hierarchy *cannot* not make sense to people who have shaped their lives around the Fiat organization. It cannot make sense to people who have moved up the Fiat ladder, one painful rung after another.

As Gary Hamel describes it, "... *if you've spend your entire life playing this massive multiplayer game called bureaucracy and learning how to accumulate and use bureaucratic power... when someone tells you, 'now I am going to change the game' is like saying to someone like LeBron James, a basketball player, that now we are going to play volleyball... probably not going to be enthusiastic about that.*"[153]

For these folks hear about co-management cannot be but *"utterly ridiculous."* They are also going to be fiercely resistant to co-ownership.

In the Interest of

The interest of a Radical company includes its financial success, of course. But that is secondary to the success of each of its co-owners, and the success of its customers, partners, providers, and whatever other communities it touches.

Financial success, yes, but not as the *only* metric.

"The interest of" a Radical company includes providing an opportunity for people to find meaning and purpose in their work and to work with a community they are aligned with and supports each other.

Radical companies are co-owned and it is *"in the interest of"* these companies that ownership be decentralized and dynamic. That ownership reflects who's contributed. Anything else would definitely not be *"in the interest of"* a Radical company.

Radical companies are co-managed. It is "*in the interest of*" these companies that there'd be no command-and-control structure, no imposed hierarchy, and a commitment to become fully transparent and decentralized. Anything else would definitely not be "*in the interest of*" a Radical company.

Juggling

It takes a lot of things to go right for a company to be successful. Venture Capital opened the door for more entrepreneurs than the system of bankers and wealthy (boys) clubs that preceded it. It's time for a new model and co-ownership can produce even more entrepreneurs and a higher rate of financial success to companies.

In a Radical company ownership is held by many co-owners, not just a select few. Co-owners directly shape the company's ownership structure, its strategy, its governance, its policies, and its operations. They have the right to fully participate in decision making, from the most trivial to the most strategic.

Not everyone *will* participate in every decision, but every co-owner has the right to. The Leadership Team practice at Nearsoft, for example, is a decision-making practice that works at scale. As always, Experiment and figure out what will work for you.

Instead of depending on one extraordinary juggler, multiple co-owners can juggle many more balls at once. And they can do it with less stress, a broader perspective, and are more likely to be financially successful in the long run.

Capital Budgeting

Besides external investments, we have to think about internal capital investments.

Retained Earnings is one such internal capital investment. It is, essentially, a piece of our profits we keep in the bank to pay for next year's basic operations and growth projects. Warren Buffet agrees that Retained Earnings are a good thing and quotes well known economist John Maynard Keynes as saying that, *"Well-managed industrial companies do not, as a rule, distribute to the shareholders the whole of their earned profits. ...*

they retain a part of their profits and put them back into the business."[154]

The more capital kept as Retained Earnings, the less capital there is to distribute as Earned Dividends and this impacts all *co-owners*. This means that unlike Fiat companies, a Radical company cannot just do this without involving *co-owners*.

One way to assure a Radical company communicates its plans and their impact to all co-owners is to insist that it returns all or most of its earnings to the co-owners, at least symbolically, to get the conversation gong.[155] Some amount of Earnings will be retained, otherwise either the company will stop growing or it would have to borrow money to grow. Nevertheless, this process must be fully transparent and intelligible to co-owners.

Somebody needs to explain why so much went into one pot versus another. Then, every team that is partaking of this capital must let the other co-owners know how they plan to invest it, why they need money-in-the-bank capital instead of a percent of cash flow, and what impact this investment is going to have on the co-owners and the company, as best they know. This would create a ritualized way for all co-owners to pay attention and really have a say about the future of the company.

This means that it is in the best interest of the company to have co-owners learn how to read the books (*e.g.*, a la Open Book Management), understand retained earnings, and learn to evaluate future plans and the impact it will have on the company and on each of them.

Resist the Voice of Fear

This also implies that, unless human nature changes dramatically overnight, plans would be more or less publicly known. This will be a recurring excuse to not disclose at least some of the plans. But keeping at least some things behind closed doors is another form of power centralization. For example, this is the approach that governments take with their *"closed doors briefings."* But as US Circuit Judge Damon Keith warned, *"Democracies die behind closed doors... When government begins closing doors, it selectively controls information rightfully belonging to the people. Selective information is misinformation.*" The same applies to Radical companies.

Resist the voice of fear. The fact that "our competition will know" is an empty scare tactic. Our competition may copy everything you do, but they cannot copy your particular co-owners. For example, Amazon decided in 2000 to switch their servers from Sun Microsystems to HP/Linux. It was one of the worst kept secrets ever and their competitors knew about it. When finished, Amazon's costs dropped dramatically

Or take the US steel industry who would not copy what the Japanese steel producers were doing to increase their productivity. The global price of steel dropped and the biggest US steel makers disappeared.

Everything about how Buurtzorg does things is well known and widely published, but others in their industries have not copied them.

At Nearsoft we've had a competitor copy many of the things we did, but to no avail. A lot of their employees preferred to become Nearsoftians and many have come over to our side of the street. Some of their clients, too, found our culture more attractive and preferable to work with and made the switch.

The other myth is that *"our clients would know."* But if you have to keep secrets from your clients, then you definitely have a more serious problem to take care of.

Liquidity

Liquidity is a form of autonomy. An ESOP account that holds wealth for me is not liquid. My bank account is.

I Need a Car

One use case is how to provide liquidity for individuals. Here's one way this could work for RADs.

I need cash to buy a car now, so I offer my RADs financial yield for a given period. This means that whoever takes me up on it would get the cash I would normally get through my RADs.

Say, for example, that I can show that my Earned Dividends are between $3,500 and $4,000 in cash every month. In six months I can expect to earn, in total, between $20,000 and $24,000. But I need to buy a car now. I offer to accept $18,000, the price of the car I want, for my RADs yield for six months.

An investor (*i.e.*, anybody inside or outside the company) takes me up on it, gives me $20,000, and I buy a used car. By the end of the six-month period, this could add up to more than 30% gross return for the investor. The return is not an interest that I pay, but comes out of the value that the company creates.

The advantage to me is that the company pays for the yield and I get the car I need sooner. For the investor, this arrangement has advantages, too,

- Because of the short period of time, the Present Value of money is not significant.
- The risk is minor because the time period is shorter and the cash generating value of the company.
- This kind of investment would require a lot less due diligence.
- It also requires much less participation by the investor.
- The quick return means that investors could recycle their gains more quickly.

At the end of five months, the investor would have no further rights to any wealth generated by my RADs. This is an investment, not a loan, and the risk that the investor takes is that the company may generate less cash than in the past (but remember that everything is transparent).

Since this all happens transparently, another investor, say, a co-worker, may offer to invest at a lower, more competitive rate (*e.g.*, $18,000 for a *five-month* lease of your RADs). Or a group of co-workers could put up an Investment Club Banner to do these types of investments on a regular basis. Or a Radical bank could do these investments very competitively. Or... you get the idea.

The Bull, Inc Exchange

SAIC was a consulting business founded by Dr Robert Beyster in 1969. Dr Beyster wanted to build a business that produced wealth for everyone, not just for him. Over time, Dr Beyster's holdings went "... *from 100 percent to 10 percent in the first year of the company's existence, and to less than 2 percent by the 1990s.*"[156] By the time he exited, the business had grown to $8B in revenue, which made Dr Beyster's 2% worth $160M.

SAIC employees were financial beneficiaries in a big way. Nevertheless, the employees were symbolic owners only because the Board and management remained in control. In the end, the Board forced Dr Beyster out of the business, sold it, and the business pretty much disappeared.

To provide liquidity for SAIC employees, as Dr Beyster explains, "... *we started up this wholly owned broker-dealer subsidiary dubbed Bull, Inc., to create a limited market in the stock and help facilitate the transfer of stock from employees who desired to sell SAIC stock to buyers,*" this gave SAIC folks "*a mechanism for buying and selling stock while remaining with SAIC.*"[157] Bull would set the stock price and "*any shareholder could offer vested stock for sale in the internal market.*"[158]

Creating Bull, Inc showed Dr Beyster's commitment to spreading wealth and ownership among SAIC's employees. He went further than most to give SAIC employees a financial stake in the business and then created Bull, Inc for liquidity. For a business that was founded in 1969, this is pretty mind blowing.

One might be tempted to think that it would be a good idea to create a similar market for Radical companies We were tempted at first, but we came to the conclusion that it doesn't make sense. RADs represent all aspects of your contribution according to your peers, not just financial value. You might have gotten some of your RADs because you took the time to talk to another co-owner when she was having a particularly bad day. How would you *trade* that?

Investment Capital

Beyond providing liquidity for individuals, we may need to provide investment capital for big company projects. Some of it might come from Retained Earnings, or a Banner, or we could borrow from *a Radical bank*.

Self-Owned Assets

Revenue, time, and even honorifics could easily be factored through RADs But what about a building or a fleet of trucks? In a Fiat business, the owner owns all assets. But since ownership is decentralized and dynamic in a Radical company, how would it work? Who gains from it? One month I may end up with 10% of all the RADs and six months later it may be 3%. If we bought the building when I was at 10%, does that mean that six months later I would own only 3% of it? One way to handle this is to have the building own itself.[159]

Imagine that we had agreed to put up a Banner that would allow us to accumulate, in three years, $5M to buy the building. Once we had the money, we would invest it to buy the building and lease it back to the company.

The percentage ownership of that investment would be determined by the number of RADs each person owns at *the time of the investment*. If I had 10% of all the allocated RADs at that point, I would own 10% of the $5M investment. If six months later my RADs went down to 3% of the total RADs, I still would own 10% of the investment that we made six months ago. This makes it easy for a co-owner to understand how much of that building she owns.

Not every member would have to participate in this investment. Others would participate for a while and then stop, or vice versa. That is OK, because each month the Banner would get money disbursed to it as a function of its RADs until we have enough to purchase the building. Maybe 10% at one point, stops, and then 2% at another time.

One possibility is to use all its dividends to pay back the $5M plus a return (see Radical Investment, below). If later on the company stops using the building, the investors could put it up for lease to another company.

RAD Leasing

A Radical company could lease RADs' yield to a capital investor.

For example, imagine a small company that needs $200,000 to buy services to get more paying customers. To do this, its co-owners would agree, for example, to have the co-owners to retain a percentage of RADs to lease to an investor.

An investor puts money up front in exchange for rights to the RADs' yield. The company uses the money to get the Cloud services it needs, it gets more paying customers, and redeems the RADs as per the terms of the agreement.

Radical Investment

A Radical investment allows the company to get a cash infusion to, say, create new products or expand into new markets. The significant difference is that a Radical investment is a purely financial transaction and includes no other rights.

The investment terms will include a risk multiplier, a timeframe, and amount for repayment. This could be something like, *"we will pay back three times the amount in three years hence,"* or *"we will pay back four times the principal amount in two years starting three years from now,"* or even *"we will pay back three times the amount if we reach X level of revenue, five times if we get to Y level of revenue, and ten times if our revenue grows beyond Z."* Again, the investor does not get any other rights other than financial.

Specifically, a Radical Investor doesn't get company stock, she doesn't get seat on the mythical Board, she doesn't get to *"fire the CEO,"* she doesn't get to demand that the company change directions, and she doesn't get to force the company to sell itself because *"revenue is not where I want it to be."* We would hope that the investor brings with her something other than money. If that's the case, the investor may become a co-owner as a valuable advisor and mentor and may be invited to discussions where her expertise and informed opinion are key. She will get RADs for contributions. But this is not a given part of the investment. Company governance remains with the co-owners, not the financial investors.

Like any investment, a Radical investment comes with the risk that things won't work out and it will not be repaid. So why do Radical investments at all?

- Every co-owner wants their business to succeed and they want to turn the investment into a blowout financial success. Their self-interest is perfectly aligned with the financial investor's interest.

- If problems arise, co-owners will be the first to recognize them. Other co-owners will know right away and in an unfiltered way (*i.e.*, transparency).

- Co-owners have the wherewithal to come up with solutions or ways around a problem.

- There is very little chance of, say, a founder taking the company in the wrong direction for long without other co-owners noticing, voicing it, and doing something about it.

Overall, a Radical investment is less risky than the traditional risk capital investment because everyone in the company, and not just a select few, know what going on viscerally, is committed to the company's success, and it is fully supportive of it.

A Radical Bank?

Since 2007 K2K Emocionando,[160] a consulting firm in Northern Spain, has helped many companies transform from Fiat management to co-management. These companies have come together as the NER Group.[161]

In 2009, the NER Group created a bank. Commercial banks were often of no help to the NER Group companies even though these banks were making plenty of money off them. When they did help, their services were expensive in spite of the fact that the NER Group companies had impeccable credit records. This became a problem during the 2010 financial crisis. In response the NER Group companies created Kutxa NER,[162] a non-profit bank capitalized by the NER companies with a small percentage of their annual revenue.

Similarly, a Radical bank would likely better serve the needs of Radical companies. Among other services, it would provide credit to these companies when needed.

Perhaps, if there had been a Radical Bank around, the co-owners of New Belgium Brewery would have not sold the company to Kirin. They might have voted against the acquisition if they had the capital to expand markets and compete with Kirin and the other international beer companies.

To be clear, a bank is not meant to stop Radical companies from failing. The bank is meant to increase their staying power and provide them with options.

Ultimately, we want to see a steady increase in the number of Radical companies. We want the Radical paradigm to become the norm and with platforms like Radical banks in place it would be more likely for this to happen.

Inactive Members

You Can Take It with You

Inactive members get to keep their RADs. However, as the number of RADs increases over time, and the inactive member's RADs will become a smaller percentage of the total RADs. They will continue to get dividends based on their RADs, but as a percentage they may get less and less over time.

Retirement

For example, imagine that when our member, Anita, goes inactive (*i.e.*, no more contributions) she has 1,000 RADs or 1% of the 100,000 RADs allocated so far. If we generate $100,000 in dividends, she gets $1,000.

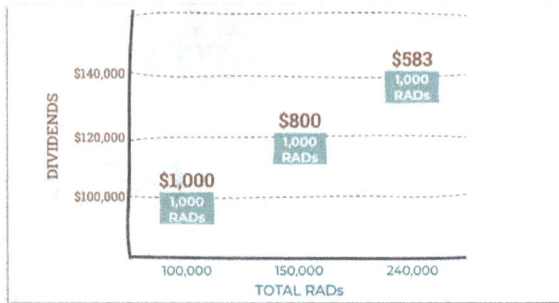

Later, the number of allocated RADs grows to 150,000 total, and dividends to $120,000. Our inactive member still has 1,000 RADs or what is now 0.67% of the total and she gets $800. Later still, the number of allocated RADs grows to 240,000 and dividends to $140,000, so she gets 0.42% of the total or $583.

You could handle differently: experiment!

Lucky!

Of course, Anita could get 'lucky,'

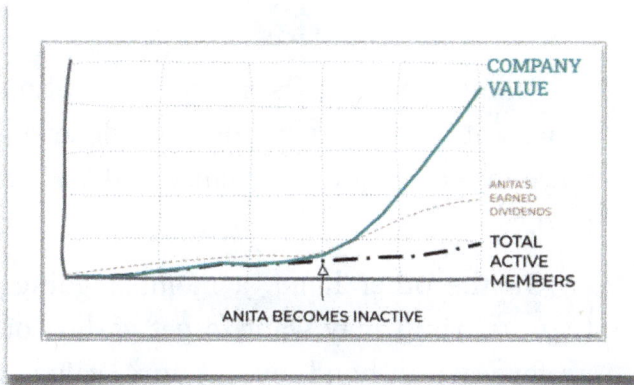

COMPANY VALUE

ANITA'S EARNED DIVIDENDS

TOTAL ACTIVE MEMBERS

ANITA BECOMES INACTIVE

But this is not really luck: she contributed to whatever made the company's value shoot up, so she deserves to benefit financially from her work. Either way, over time Anita's contributions are less significant, her percentage of allocated RADs goes down, and her RADs' yield reflects that.

The community may decide a different policy. Take your local pizza parlor or favorite small restaurant. In these cases, it may make more sense to set it up so that the factoring value of RADs of inactive members goes down over time. For example, if active members get $1 as a dividend for every RAD in a given month, an inactive member would get 50¢ after being inactive for 24 months, 25¢ after 36 months, and zero after 60 months.

Cashing Out?

Selling your RADs is not an option. RADs represent your contributions and determines your voice in matters of governance and that cannot be sold.

On the other hand, a member going inactive (*e.g.*, retiring) may want to get cashed out: she'd prefer cash-in-hand over future value. Another option is for the company to retire her RADs in exchange for a predictable monthly payout. We can imagine other alternatives, but, as always, experiment.

Note that this cashing out remains a financial transaction.

Who's Inactive?

This brings up the question of who can be considered inactive? Is there a criteria?

Full-time and *part-time* are not useful. *On payroll* or not doesn't make sense, either. We think one criteria could be based on whether or not a member receives RADs at Distributions. If a member does not receive any RADs for a number of cycles in a row, then she could be considered inactive. Even somebody who works every day could lose his governance rights if he has not made any contributions (*i.e.*, received no RADs) for a while.

On the other hand, somebody who contributes once a month and gets RADs is an active member.

As always the answer is that there is no right answer and you'll have to experiment to find out who is considered inactive in your case.

Coming up Next

Outgoing: Fiat

The Fiat dogma goes something like this: There is, and always has been, a hierarchy of power that rules every aspect of our being, our society, and our world. Without it, we'd be nothing but wild beasts. Men rule over women, adults rule over children, the armed rule over the defenseless, the powerful rules over the weak, and the gods rule over us all. Our superiors order us about as they see fit, and we happily obey; then we do the same to our subordinates and expect the same obedience.

This mindset is pervasive and invisible, like water to the proverbial fish.

Every aspect of our world is born of it. *"Today's capitalist economic order is a monstrous cosmos, into which the individual is born and which in practice is for him, at least as an individual, simply a given, an immutable shell..., in which he is obliged to live."*[163] This is what German sociologist Max Weber wrote in 1905, more than 100 years ago. This immutable shell is slowly imploding and will crush us unless we find alternatives.

Before Copernicus, the dogma of the time had planet Earth at the center of the known Universe. Copernicus moved the Sun to the center instead.

He set Earth rotating around it and showed us an expanding Universe.

According to the Fiat dogma, capital, ownership, and power are fused together. He who has the capital is the owner and has the power. That is how the story goes. Breaking apart capital, ownership, and power is going to be harder than moving the Sun and Earth, but we'll have to do it one way or the other. We need a different paradigm, one that puts all of us at the center and lets us all thrive.

Emerging: Radical

People are *co-owners* of the company and expect to know about and have a say on major ownership decisions that affect them. This applies to strategic decisions with any impact on the people who embody the company.

People are capable of *co-managing* to get things done because they have the skills to do it. That's what they learned at home and school. They've heard stories of bosses and such, but those feel like tales from a cheap dystopian novel.

People are sensitive to any obstacle that gets in the way of doing *meaningful* work, the voice to point them out, the imagination to find ways around them, and the individual and social skills to remove them.

People join teams because they feel aligned with their explicit impact and purpose. They know they can contribute to the team's mission and want to be part of it, want to *belong* to it. They have learned to "*tell their truths, take responsibility, and accept accountability,*"[164] individually and as teams.

People have the sensitivity to see when *transparency* or *decentralization* are being blocked. They are committed to removing these blocks so that we can continue to make progress.

People have the confidence to experiment and the capacity to learn from the results. They have learned to come together and work towards an explicit Purpose to make an Impact on the world.

Make It the Norm

We want the Radical paradigm to become the norm. We want to see co-owned and co-managed companies become the norm, places where people come to work together and share the result of their effort equitably. The training grounds for people to craft their own paths, make collaboration a habit, and own their destinies. What people learn at *their* companies will then spread to our homes, our schools, our communities, and eventually to a world *"more natural, organic, yet maybe evolutionary."*[165]

Human nature resists the unknown, and the suggestions in this book will be seen as suspicious at best.

We hope that this book has helped give shape to an *"insight which was already yours."*

> Change is possible because it is necessary
>
> — *John Zerzan*

Endnotes

1   Renamed Encora Nearshore by the time you read this. https://www.encora.com

2   For more references, see DOT-COM Bubble. https://radicals.world/nO7aTa

3   Ben Geier. What Did We Learn From the Dotcom Stock Bubble of 2000?. March 12, 2015 https://radicals.world/lFa66V (alt. https://diigo.com/Ohodmv)

4   Marc Andreessen. Why Software is Eating the World. August 20, 2011. https://radicals.world/QlhBnv (alt, https://diigo.com/Oi9uli).

5   For more references, see The Year 2000 Problem. https://radicals.world/uVFlnV

6   Based on Trancept Systems), founded by Nick England, Mary Whitton, and Tim Van Hook. Sun acquired Trancept as an acquihire, before that name came into vogue. https://radicals.world/o3i8Aw (alt, https://diigo.com/Oimaks)

7   Sun Microsystems Inc 10-K Annual Report. https://radicals.world/9nBgPx (alt, https://diigo.com/Og43oz)

8   Today we would call this a time-boxed release. Obvious as it may sound now, the idea was fairly new back then. James Martin had already written about it in 1991 in his book, Rapid Application Development. https://radicals.world/Y7veoI

9   Chuck Blakeman. Rehumanizing the Workplace. 2020. https://radicals.world/OQOOzs

10   See The Global Financial Crisis in 2009 for more references. https://radicals.world/RPNprB

11   See The Force for more references. https://radicals.world/awOOpg

12   For more references, see Maverick. https://radicals.world/M3x22N

13   Logan et al. Tribal Leadership. June 7, 2011. https://radicals.world/me9oOC

[14] Chip Conley. PEAK. 2007. https://radicals.world/JHgvVR

[15] Matthew Kelly. The Dream Manager. 2007. https://radicals.world/rxaJVU

[16] Dennis Bakke. The Advice Process. 2012. https://youtu.be/vUaDD9mnXVI?t=24

[17] For more information, see Nothing About Us Without Us. https://en.wikipedia.org/wiki/Nothing_About_Us_Without_Us

[18] David Marquette. Leadership Nudge developing trust in one another– Above and Below the Waterline. The term seems to have originated with W L Gore and Associates. https://radicals.world/3UM9hu

[19] Elinor Ostrom. Lee Kuan Yew School of Public Policy – Beyond Markets and States. 2010. https://youtu.be/E5ZPGeF2ics?t=625

[20] Douglas McGregor. The Human Side of Enterprise. 1975. For a summary, see appendix Theory X, Theory Y. https://radicals.world/cNbgKp (alt, https://diigo.com/Ofnzpe)

[21] NetMBA Business Knowledge Center. Theory X and Theory Y. https://radicals.world/1w2VQb (alt, http://www.netmba.com/mgmt/ob/motivation/mcgregor/)

[22] Douglas McGregor. The Human Side of Enterprise, p 2. 1975. https://radicals.world/cNbgKp (alt, https://diigo.com/Ofnzpe)

[23] State of the Global Workplace. Gallop Report, 2017. https://www.diigo.com/item/pdf/zk1n/1xpv

[24] Paul Buchheit, engineer, entrepreneur, investor, ex-Sun Microsystem, creator of Gmail, and ex-Facebook. https://radicals.world/xoDqyt

[25] Umair Haque, Betterness – Economics for Humans. https://a.co/3q3Hlrv

[26] Catherine Clifford. Hedge fund billionaire Ray Dalio: Capitalism basically is not working for the majority of people." CNBC's Make It, Jan 16, 2019. https://radicals.world/I2mCJ7 (alt, https://diigo.com/Oi9udg)

27 This attitude has been called "business unionism" by James Dennis Hoff in 'No Power Greater:' Solidarity and Struggle at CUNY. It has also been called the "common good" view by Alan Gillies in Software Quality: Theory and Management. https://radicals.world/kUAh1U (alt, https://diigo.com/Oh2O7e) https://radicals.world/U3flll (alt. https://radicals.world/nOcpxN)

28 Tyson Yunkaporta. Sand Talk. 2020. https://a.co/5zWVdrk

29 Mark Carney, governor of the Bank of England. By invitation: Mark Carney on how the economy must yield to human values. 2020. https://radicals.world/b75wQ7 (alt, https://diigo.com/Oimae3)

30 Peter Leeson. The Invisible Hook: The Hidden Economics of Pirates. 2009. https://a.co/3H78JQV

31 For more references, see Post-World War II economic expansion. https://radicals.world/qXYLAy

32 Scott Bader Constitution. https://radicals.world/5BXSNh (alt, https://www.diigo.com/user/matt_perez/b/547882995)

33 The Gore Story. https://radicals.world/eJIK7k (alt, https://diigo.com/Oi9udl)

34 Bernhard Schroeder. What Is the Magic Number of Employees in a Startup or Company, in One Location, Before Tribalism Begins to Break It Apart?. Feb 2020. https://radicals.world/Fslg4k (alt, https://diigo.com/Oiejxh)

35 Gary Hamel. Building an Innovation Democracy, p 9. https://radicals.world/WckPSC (alt, https://www.diigo.com/item/pdf/zk1n/9cn3)

36 Gary Hamel. Innovation Democracy: W.L. Gore's Original Management Model. 2010. https://radicals.world/pZ3CId (alt, https://diigo.com/Oiejxm)

37 James Huston. The American and British Debate Over Equality, 1776-1920 (Kindle). 2017. https://a.co/1PtmemO

38 The Electoral College had no legitimate purpose once the 13 Amendment was adopted. https://radicals.world/xvVEHg https://radicals.world/WrvSoC

39 Dr Joseph Blasi. A Founding Father Profit Sharing Fix for Inequality. April 14, 2017. https://radicals.world/bW7MUU (alt, https://diigo.com/0imafl)

40 Peter Drucker, Management: Tasks, Responsibilities, Practices. 1973. https://radicals.world/tGgi8I

41 Kim Jordan, in an interview by Lucas Li. New Belgium Brewing tour + interview with CEO Kim Jordan. Nov 14, 2011. https://radicals.world/tBw5tK (alt, https://diigo.com/0h1qo7)

42 The New Belgium ESOP was first established in 2000 when it owned 35% of the company. In 2005 it owned 42%, 47% in 2012, and in 2017 the ESOP became the sole owner of the company.

43 The Foundation for Enterprise Development. Directed by Passage Productions (52 minute). We the Owners: Employees Expanding the American Dream, a film by Infobase Learning / Films Media Group. https://radicals.world/SQPLB2

44 Ironically, in 1917 Russia had the smallest proletariat in all of Europe. Most of their population was eking a living off the land, not working in factories.

45 For more references, see Henry George. https://radicals.world/0dFYy9

46 For the original, see Progress and Poverty. https://radicals.world/qburBQ https://www.diigo.com/item/pdf/zk1n/qh70

47 For more references, see San Yat-sen. https://radicals.world/SZIPs1

48 For more references see Henry George. Progress and Poverty. 1879. https://www.diigo.com/item/pdf/zk1n/qh70

49 Francis Peddle, PhD, Philosophies of Integration: Sun Yat-Sen and Henry George. https://radicals.world/ncBKEC

50 Pierre Lemieux. Land Taxes: The Return of Henry George. 2018. https://radicals.world/cZc5p6 (alt, https://www.econlib.org/land-taxes-the-return-of-henry-george/)

51 See Lizzie Magie for more references. https://radicals.world/Q12lGp

52 Lizzie J Magie. The Landlord's Game. Patented Jan 5, 1904. https://radicals.world/5ybTQl (alt, https://diigo.com/Oi9uer)

53 Remarks of Honorable Charles Eckert of Pennsylvania in the House of Representatives. Eckert, Henry George – Sound Economics and the 'New Deal.' Tuesday, July 2, 1931. https://radicals.world/o84Yrz (alt, https://www.diigo.com/item/pdf/zk1n/tybj)

54 Remarks of Honorable Charles Eckert of Pennsylvania in the House of Representatives. Eckert, Henry George – Sound Economics and the 'New Deal.' Tuesday, July 2, 1931. https://radicals.world/NjQS37 (alt, https://www.diigo.com/item/pdf/zk1n/tybj)

55 Remarks of Honorable Charles Eckert of Pennsylvania in the House of Representatives. Eckert, Henry George – Sound Economics and the 'New Deal.' Tuesday, July 2, 1931. https://radicals.world/NjQS37 (alt, https://www.diigo.com/item/pdf/zk1n/tybj)

56 Remarks of Honorable Charles Eckert of Pennsylvania in the House of Representatives. Eckert, Henry George – Sound Economics and the 'New Deal.' Tuesday, July 2, 1931. https://radicals.world/NjQS37 (alt, https://www.diigo.com/item/pdf/zk1n/tybj)

57 See, Georgism for more references. https://radicals.world/XhT9wT (alt, https://diigo.com/Oiig3b)

58 Annika Neklason. The 140-Year-Old Dream of "Government Without Taxation." income after it's produced Atlantic, April 15, 2019. https://radicals.world/ceAbXD (alt, https://diigo.com/Ojrtrn)

59 Louis O Kelso, Interview in July 1983. https://radicals.world/Qq3AaQ

60 The Foundation for Enterprise Development. Directed by Passage Productions (52 minute). We the Owners: Employees Expanding the American Dream, a film by Infobase Learning / Films Media Group. https://youtu.be/6sszYBw8tYo?t=106

61 Seth Godin. What kind of org?. May 4, 2020. https://radicals.world/Wl06ji (alt, https://seths.blog/2020/05/what-kind-of-org/)

62 That is what as \ written widely, but I have not personally verified it.

63 Valve: Handbook for New Employees. https://radicals.world/JMfg2K (alt, https://diigo.com/0gta1p)

64 Joost Minnaar. The World's Most Pioneering Company of Our Times. Corporate Rebels, 2018. https://radicals.world/IIEJpD (alt, https://diigo.com/0hfysm)

65 Chuck Blakeman is the author of Making Money Is Killing Your Business and Why Employees Are Always a Bad Idea. https://radicals.world/4Xx2G8 (alt, https://radicals.world/LM14eE)

66 Jing Hu and Jacob Hirsh. Accepting Lower Salaries for Meaningful Work. Frontiers in Psychology, 29 September 2017. You can find lots of similar works online. https://radicals.world/27ufgg (alt, https://radicals.world/980PFP)

67 Alexandra Anderson. Twitter post. May 9, 2020. https://twitter.com/alexandersonmd/status/1259327416926908423

68 Nilofer Merchant. Should You Say No to that Big Job Offer?. Feb 4, 2020. https://radicals.world/pYrd9D (alt, https://radicals.world/GUBzQa)

69 Brené Brown. The power of vulnerability. TEDxHouston. 2010. https://radicals.world/uy3lKE

70 Nilofer Merchant. Should You Say No to that Big Job Offer?. Feb 4, 2020. https://radicals.world/pYrd9D (alt, https://radicals.world/OTZ3Vm)

71 This is also a gesture popularized in The Hunger Games movies to express unity with people striving to survive. Since 2014 it has also become a symbol of pro-democracy in Thailand. Very apropos. https://en.wikipedia.org/wiki/The_Hunger_Games https://radicals.world/pG9bAM (alt, https://diigo.com/0iu409

72 Luke Hohman. Innovation Games: Prune the Product Tree. For how we played the game at Nearsoft, see Prune the Product Tree. https://www.innovationgames.com/prune-the-product-tree/

[73] Luis Ortiz. Work Hard, Have Fun: a Day-in-the-Life at Nearsoft. 2016. https://nearsoft.com/videos/life-at-nearsoft/ (alt, https://diigo.com/Oj6zps)

[74] See appendix Recruiting for more references.

[75] Jessica Sillman, quoting Phil Rosedale in Why Employees Should Decide Who Gets Bonuses. https://radicals.world/t1P8ht (alt, https://diigo.com/Oh1Oy6)

[76] James Owen. Drawing Out the Dragons: A Meditation on Art, Destiny, and the Power of Choice. 2014. https://radicals.world/KjVrI5

[77] Jessica Sillman, quoting Phil Rosedale in Why Employees Should Decide Who Gets Bonuses. https://radicals.world/KjVrI5 (alt, https://www.diigo.com/user/matt_perez/b/574995418)

[78] Sanford DeVoe, Sheena Iyengar. Medium of Exchange Matters: What's Fair for Goods Is Unfair for Money. 2010. https://radicals.world/KjVrI5 (alt, https://www.diigo.com/user/matt_perez/b/574995418)

[79] Michael R A Chance. Social Fabrics of the Mind, Michael R A Chance, Ed. 2015. https://a.co/7pip7pR

[80] Michael R A Chance. Social Fabrics of the Mind, Michael R A Chance, Ed. 2015. https://a.co/ivUwBf9

[81] Michael R A Chance. Social Fabrics of the Mind, Michael R A Chance, Ed. 2015. https://a.co/2IwsOyt

[82] Michael R A Chance. Social Fabrics of the Mind, Michael R A Chance, Ed. 2015. https://a.co/2PSFmPh

[83] Chuck Blakeman. Rehumanizing the Workplace by Giving Everybody Their Brain Back. 2020. https://radicals.world/kegSnn

[84] Jack Rimington. Twitter post. Feb 5, 2020. https://radicals.world/IgOfJa

[85] Seth Godin. Born to run (things) alt., here). Jan 14, 2021. https://seths.blog/2021/01/born-to-run-things/ (alt, https://diigo.com/Ojgole)

86 Jack Stack, The Great Game of Business. https://youtu.be/SOqw_GX8I5A?t=431

87 Jack Stack, The Great Game of Business. https://youtu.be/SOqw_GX8I5A?t=431

88 Ricardo Semler, Maverick. 1988. https://radicals.world/ANgLYQ

89 Jie Li, Bruce Boghosian, and Chengli Li. The Affine Wealth Model: An agent-based model of asset exchange that allows for negative-wealth agents and its empirical validation. 2018. https://radicals.world/ntlTXw (alt, https://www.diigo.com/item/pdf/zk1n/2x59)

290 Bruce M Boghosian, Is Inequality Inevitable?. November 2019. https://radicals.world/xI17kA (alt, https://diigo.com/Ofsqtw)

91 Bernard Lietaer, Jacqui Dunne. Rethinking Money: How New Currencies Turn Scarcity into Prosperity. 2013. https://a.co/954O96N

92 Larry Elliott. Richest 62 people as wealthy as half of the world's population, says Oxfam. 2016. Dylan Matthew. Are 26 billionaires worth more than half the planet? The debate, explained Jan 22, 2019. https://radicals.world/BmkTQ5 https://radicals.world/pKM4NR

93 See Fagor for more references. https://en.wikipedia.org/wiki/Fagor

94 BuurtzorgT website. https://radicals.world/hIDLRS

95 Joost Minnaar. How to Rapidly Scale a Mission-Driven Company without Selling Out. October 2020. https://radicals.world/kzy8j7

96 Steward-ownership. Purpose Foundation site. https://radicals.world/mXBU3C

97 ESOP (Employee Stock Ownership Plan) Facts. https://radicals.world/35OpGH (alt, https://diigo.com/Oibkhg)

98 WorldBlu's Freedom at Work model. https://radicals.world/35OpGH (alt, https://radicals.world/45G5wX)

99 ESOP (Employee Stock Ownership Plan) Facts. https://radicals.world/35OpGH (alt, https://diigo.com/Oibkhi)

100 Bernard Paranque and Hugh Willmott. Cooperatives: Saviours or Gravediggers of Capitalism? The ambivalent case of the John Lewis Partnership. 2014. https://radicals.world/ElFHKk (alt, https://www.diigo.com/user/matt_perez/b/545671545)

101 Nikil Saval. Utopia, Abandoned. August 29, 2019. https://radicals.world/apwgQc (alt, https://diigo.com/Oipwxj)

102 Sociocratic Democracy. https://radicals.world/W3ny8W (alt, https://diigo.com/Oipwya)

103 Gerard Enderberg, as quoted in Beyond the Bottom Line: Socially Innovative Business Owners. https://a.co/1gc5YIT

104 Edward Albert Filene. https://radicals.world/gJXwrb (alt, https://diigo.com/Ojc3xr)

105 Jack Quarter. Beyond the Bottom Line: Socially Innovative Business Owners. 2000. https://a.co/f4qTN3u

106 Mary Parker Follett. The New State. 1918. https://a.co/h8Berdd

107 Elinor Ostrom – Facts. The Nobel Prize site. https://radicals.world/izty4z (alt, https://diigo.com/Oia7y5)

108 Dr Paul Atkins, course material. PROSOCIAL Facilitator Certification. 2019. https://radicals.world/uhEMi7

109 Franz de Waal. Two Monkeys Were Paid Unequally. Apr 4, 2013. https://radicals.world/dOgzRK

110 Most of the HR folks are genuinely good people who went into this role to help others. Indeed, they very often are the ones who lead implementation of good, high impact programs. In the end, though, their job is to shield the business and top execs from lawsuits.

111 James Barker. Tightening the Iron Cage: Concertive Control in Self-Managing Teams. Administrative Science Quarterly, Vol 38, No 3, Sep 1993. https://radicals.world/wFNe3c (alt, https://www.diigo.com/user/matt_perez/b/545734494)

112 Richard Bartlett. Bootstrapping a bossless organisation in 3 easy steps ;-). May 19, 2016. https://radicals.world/bAJsmz (alt, https://diigo.com/Oia7re)

[113] J Kim Wright. Lawyers as Changemakers: The Global Integrative Law Movement. year. https://a.co/eLM7JKw

[114] Zulema Salinas. Twitter Post. Aug 19, 2020. https://radicals.world/Ohdf5J

[115] Robert Kegan. The Further Reaches of Adult Development – Robert Kegan. YouTube, https://radicals.world/7YX6h3

[116] David Klein A Brief History of American K-12 Mathematics Education in the 20th Century. 2003. Emphasis added. https://radicals.world/Ws9frS

[117] The whole "mind-body problem" is coming under scrutiny and my sense is that it's time to retire it. See the works of Dr Georg Northoff and others. https://radicals.world/V8ZDF6

[118] Emphasis added. Geert Hofstede. Dimensionalizing Culture, The Hofstede Model in Context. 2011. As Hofstede has said many times, this is a measure of culture at the national level and makes no claims below that, certainly not at the individual level. https://radicals.world/Q6XnLF (alt, https://www.diigo.com/item/pdf/zk1n/bjr2#)

[119] Pablo Aretxabala. Las 10 estructuras básicas de la autogestión nuestro NERbyK2K. Jul 24, 2020. https://radicals.world/28Izg8 (alt, https://diigo.com/0iezem)

[120] Joost Minnaar. VkusVill: How A Russian Giant Disrupts The Retail Industry. Corporate Rebels Blog Jan 2, 2021. https://corporate-rebels.com/vkusvill/

[121] Ved Krishna. Nature Based Packaging. TEDxPSITKanpur, March 24, 2018. https://youtu.be/cxQc6Mz_c3U?t=41

[122] Pradeep Chakravarthy. Management & Leadership: Lesson from Temples. July 9, 2019. https://www.youtube.com/watch?v=ak6avSgOCEE

[123] Suresh Pandit. https://www.linkedin.com/in/sureshpandit/

[124] James Barker. Tightening the Iron Cage: Concertive Control in Self-Managing Teams, p 3. 1993. https://radicals.world/5eO2C9 (alt, https://www.diigo.com/user/matt_perez/b/545734494)

125 Richard Edwards. Contested Terrain: The Transformation of the Workplace in the Twentieth Century, p 22. 1979. Emphasis adde https://radicals.world/skz6a3 (alt, https://radicals.world/l8qAZS)

126 Gary Hamel and Michele Zanini. Humanocracy (Kindle). 2020. https://a.co/cSy5PSK

127 Jonathan Haidt. The Righteous Mind. March 13, 2012. http://a.co/3Z6EDHK

128 Tyson Yunkaporta. Sand Talks: How Indigenous Thinking Can Save the Word. May 2020. https://a.co/ObVttP2

129 Richard Sheridan. Joy, Inc: How We Built a Workplace People Love, p 3. 2013. https://a.co/dmpCgNX

130 John Holloway. Change the World Without Taking Power. 2013. https://a.co/ivS7wlx

131 Gallup Report. State of the Global Workplace. 2017. https://radicals.world/UjEXuV (alt, https://www.diigo.com/user/matt_perez/b/537244593)

132 Dr M Hayes, Dr F Chumney, Dr C Wright, M Buckingham. The Global Study of Engagement Technical Report. 2019. https://radicals.world/ib5OvR (alt, https://www.diigo.com/item/pdf/zk1n/w6g1)

133 Doug Kirkpatrick, author of: Beyond Empowerment, 2017; From Hierarchy to High Performance, 2018; The No-Limits Enterprise, 2019; Essays from the Edge, 2020. https://radicals.world/YUSRh8 https://radicals.world/j76Iqu https://radicals.world/6jFr3D https://radicals.world/JyhC75

134 Doug Kirkpatrick. Interactive Periodic Table of the Future of Work. https://radicals.world/1B2TH7

135 Umair Haque. Betterness: Economics for Humans. 2011. https://a.co/5gfGxjl

136 Lisa Gill interviews Gary Hamel on Busting Bureaucracy for Good in her podcast Leadermorphosis. https://radicals.world/gTNXVl (alt, https://radicals.world/XWnF7f)

[137] Frederic Laloux's response in the comments to Bursting the Bubble: Teal Ain't Real. https://radicals.world/535gKO (alt, https://www.diigo.com/item/pdf/zk1n/cliy)

[138] SenseTribe mentions it in their Guide and the Great Game of Business movement talks about it, too. https://radicals.world/yfv9tp https://radicals.world/MVbHCq

[139] Seth Godin. When can we talk about our systems? (alt. here). September 24, 2020. https://radicals.world/E46PwG (alt, https://diigo.com/Oijnru)

[140] Nilofer Merchant. Should You Say No to that Big Job Offer? Feb 4, 2020. https://radicals.world/NAbUVW

[141] Mike Moyer. Slicing Pie website. https://radicals.world/Vi9ZCF

[142] Mike Moyer, Slicing Pie at Stanford University. https://youtu.be/pLGDba8aSWE?t=225

[143] Mike Moyer. Slicing Pie at Stanford University. Mar 17, 2014. https://youtu.be/pLGDba8aSWE?t=3809

[144] Mike Moyer. Slicing Pie at Stanford University. Mar 17, 2014. https://youtu.be/pLGDba8aSWE?t=3254

[145] Slicing Pie, Version 2.3. Page 128 (70%).

[146] Bram van der Lecq. No More Ass-Kissing: An Alternative Salary Model. Corporate Rebels blog, 2020. https://radicals.world/OEAqzu (alt, https://diigo.com/Oipx52)

[147] Nicolas di Tada. Salary compensations without intermediation. Manas Blog, Dec 13, 2018. https://radicals.world/B4Jolk (alt, https://diigo.com/Ohjq18)

[148] Pim de Morree, Corporate Rebels. Self-Set Salaries: A Practical Guide. 2018. https://corporate-rebels.com/self-set-salaries/

[149] Maciej Gałkiewicz. What I've learned as a CEO from a year of self-set salaries. May 8, 2018. https://radicals.world/SPbBOb (alt, https://diigo.com/Oipx5r)

[150] Liqueed, Happyforce, 10Pines, Basetis, Manas. https://radicals.world/ml9YQO https://radicals.world/JWLYDK https://radicals.world/yQixnw https://radicals.world/SVV6RG https://manas.tech/

[151] Tom Peters. Twitter post. Aug 2, 2017. https://twitter.com/matt_perez/status/892850058428911618

[152] Edmund Burke. Reflections on the Revolution in France [PDF]. https://radicals.world/5oY7Tu

[153] Lisa Gill interviews Gary Hamel on Busting Bureaucracy for Good, 9:40.https://radicals.world/PeVZ7x (alt, https://www.youtube.com/watch?v=Q4X_JuTtwjg&t=494s)

[154] Warren Buffet, Chairman. Letter to 2019 Berkshire's Shareholders. February 22, 2020. https://radicals.world/qTd8Om (alt, https://www.diigo.com/item/pdf/zkln/3y78)

[155] Louis O Kelso, Mortimer Adler. The Capitalist Manifesto. 1958. https://radicals.world/W1HncK

[156] Dr J Robert Beyster, Peter Economy. The SAIC Solution: Built by Employee Owners. May 28, 2014. https://a.co/dkEwTbK

[157] Dr J Robert Beyster, Peter Economy. The SAIC Solution: Built by Employee Owners. May 28, 2014. http://a.co/8N2369p

[158] Dr J Robert Beyster, Peter Economy. The SAIC Solution: Built by Employee Owners. May 28, 2014. https://a.co/glwHCcS

[159] This idea comes directly from Joeri Torfs and Pim Ampe.

[160] K2K Emocionando. https://radicals.world/KozIZu

[161] The NER Group. NER stands for Nuevo Estilo de Relaciones or New Style of Relationships. This "new style" is very close to what we call co-management. https://radicals.world/tEaXbr

[162] Pronounced kut-cha. See Carmen Larrakoetxea's NER Group crea Kutxa NER, un modelo de financiación empresarial alternativo a los bancos. El Economista, March 3, 2015. https://radicals.world/EwGRNp (alt, https://diigo.com/0irvcd)

[163] Max Weber. The Protestant Ethic and the Spirit of Capitalism and Other Writings. 1905. Translated by Peter Baehr and Gordon Wells. https://a.co/4yig0e8

[164] Thanks to J Kim Wright for the thought, so beautifully expressed. Private communications.

[165] Bruce Peters, private communication.

www.ingramcontent.com/pod-product-compliance
Lightning Source LLC
Chambersburg PA
CBHW061158240326
R18026600001B/R180266PG41519CBX00033B/9